Caroline F Cutler

**Primary Manual Training**

Methods in Form Study, Clay, Paper and Color Work

Caroline F Cutler

**Primary Manual Training**

*Methods in Form Study, Clay, Paper and Color Work*

ISBN/EAN: 9783337059439

Printed in Europe, USA, Canada, Australia, Japan

Cover: Foto ©Thomas Meinert / pixelio.de

More available books at www.hansebooks.com

# METHODS IN FORM STUDY, CLAY, PAPER AND COLOR WORK.

---

### BY CAROLINE F. CUTLER,

*Lucretia Crocker School, Boston.*
*Special Instructor in Manual Training to the Primary Teachers of Boston.*

BOSTON AND CHICAGO:
EDUCATIONAL PUBLISHING COMPANY.
1891.

## Publishers' Note.

The author presents, in plain language, *practical methods* of teaching Manual Training in primary schools.

In fact, this book is but a transcript of the regular work done by the author in her own school, and no plans have been suggested that cannot be readily accomplished by the average pupil.

After the school committee of Boston had added to the course of study for the primary schools, a course in *Manual Training*, the author was summoned by the committee to give instruction to the primary teachers in the methods to be employed in teaching Modeling in Clay, Paper-cutting and Folding, Stick-laying, etc.

The line of instruction was in strict harmony with the course of study, and this book, which is the epitome of her instruction, is issued in response to the demands of many teachers.

# CONTENTS.

|  | PAGE |
|---|---|
| General Suggestions, . . . . . . . | V. |
| Plan of Development of each Type-Solid, . . . | VII. |
| The Sphere, . . . . . . . . | 5 |
| The Cube, . . . . . . . . | 13 |
| Paper-Folding, *Series I*, . . . . . . | 22 |
| Paper-Folding — Forms of Life, . . . . | 32 |
| Paper-Folding — Cutting and Pasting, . . . | 35 |
| The Cylinder, . . . . . . . . | 38 |
| Review of First Three Solids, . . . . . | 45 |
| Color, . . . . . . . . . | 46 |
| Paper-Cutting — Color Work, . . . . . | 53 |
| The Hemisphere, . . . . . . . | 57 |
| The Square Prism, . . . . . . . | 62 |
| The Right-Angled Triangular Prism, . . . | 66 |
| Equilateral Triangular Prism, . . . . . | 69 |
| Paper-Folding, *Series II*, . . . . . . | 75 |
| Dimensions, . . . . . . . . | 89 |
| The Ellipsoid, . . . . . . . . | 93 |
| The Oblate Spheroid, . . . . . . . | 99 |
| The Ovoid, . . . . . . . . | 100 |
| The Cone, . . . . . . . . | 107 |
| The Square Pyramid, . . . . . . . | 113 |
| The Equilateral Triangular Pyramid, . . . . | 120 |
| Suggestions for connecting Manual Training with other Studies, . . . | 122 |
| Constructive Work in Card-board. . . . . | 124 |
| Suggestions for Stick-Laying, . . . . | 128 |

# General Suggestions.

CLAY.— Modeling clay may be obtained at the Pottery Works, or of a plaster image-maker, at a cost not exceeding three cents per pound.

Buy the *moist* clay, and by keeping it in a covered earthen jar, with a damp cloth *over the clay*, it will be ready for instant use. After each lesson, preserve the best specimens, and always moisten the clay before returning it to the jar.

Clay is generally so dry and hard, after the children have used it, that "simple moistening" may not be enough. It is best then to put it in a dish, and cover it with water.

After it has thus stood a few hours, or until thoroughly softened, pour off the water, and wrap the clay in a large cloth. Place the clay thus wrapped upon a plane surface, as a slate or a board, and knead, turning it in different directions, till the water is thoroughly pressed out and a compact mass formed, when it will be in condition to be returned to the jar for future use.

Clay may be cut by means of a knife, wire or strong thread. Thread is better for children's use than wire, as the latter is apt to

## GENERAL SUGGESTIONS.

twist and become uneven. Thin, stiff cards can be used to cut small pieces of clay.

Clay may be modeled by rolling between the palms of the hands or upon a plane surface, and by striking it gently upon a plane surface.

A sharp-pointed stick — (A wooden tooth-pick, for instance), may be used to draw lines upon the clay. A stick with a rough end may be used to puncture the clay, to give a rough surface to the background.

PAPER.— Manilla paper in sheets, measuring 24 x 36 and weighing thirty pounds to the ream, is "about right" for paper-folding, as it will be found thin enough to fold readily.

This paper may be bought by the single pound, and the dealer will cut it into squares of any desired size. Four-inch squares are commonly used, though large squares will be needed for certain forms.

Thin card-board or development paper, should be used in the representation of solids in the higher classes.

Development paper 24 × 36, weighs about eighty pounds to the ream.

Manilla paper may be used *for drawing* in primary schools, but it should be of heavier quality than the folding paper. Paper should be furnished liberally to the children that they may become accustomed to using it freely in preference to the slate.

Colored paper cut in four-inch squares, may be purchased by the package, or, it may be bought by the sheet, and cut to order.

TABLETS. — Tablets of various sizes and shapes for use in form study, may be *purchased*, but if they are too expensive, satisfactory tablets can be made of card or stiff paper. The children can make them by tracing around the edge of a pattern and then cutting out the forms.

STICK-LAYING.— Colored sticks are sold for this purpose, but splints, or even wooden tooth picks may be used.

SCISSORS.— Short blunt-pointed scissors are the best for young children to use.

PASTING.— Each child should have a little plate containing a small quantity of paste. A few children may be taught to fill the plates, and distribute them quickly. A wooden tooth-pick is better than a brush for applying paste.

CARD-PRICKING.— Pricking cushions and pins are prepared for Kindergarten use. Draw any desired pattern upon paper and place the paper over the card to be sewed. At suitable intervals along the outline of the pattern prick holes through paper and card. Remove the paper and the card is ready for sewing. If the cushions and pins cannot readily be obtained, place the card upon a piece of thick flannel and prick with a large shawl pin.

Each subject of form study may be systematically developed by following the plan here suggested.

1. The study of the facts of the type-solid.
2. Modeling type-solid of clay.
3. Modeling objects based upon the type-solid.

GENERAL SUGGESTIONS.

4. Half solid, and objects based upon it.
5. Study of views of type-solid, with the tablet exercises.
6. Tracing on clay tablets.
7. Sewing-cards.
8. Plane of the type-solid.
9. Paper-folding and cutting.
10. Stick-laying (where there are straight edges.)
11. Arm and pencil-movements.
12. Drawing of objects based upon the type-solid.

## PLAN FOR DEVELOPING THE SPHERE.

1. Study the facts of the type-solid. . . . See page 5
2. Model a sphere of clay. . . . " 6
3. Model clay objects based upon the sphere. . " 6
4. Cut the clay sphere. Hemispheres. . " 7
5. Place tablets. . . . . . . " 8
6. Sewing-cards. . . . . . . " 9, 10
7. Arm and pencil-movements. . . . " 11, 12
8. Draw free-hand circle. . . . . " 12
9. Draw outline of objects based upon the sphere. " 12

## GENERAL SUGGESTIONS.

### PLAN FOR DEVELOPING THE CUBE.

1. Compare with the sphere and study the facts of type-solid. . . . . . . See page 13
2. Model cube of clay. . . . . " 14
3. Model objects based upon the cube. . . " 14
4. Make a paper cube. . . . " 14
5. Faces of cube from the type-solid. . " 16
6. Tablet exercises. . . . . . " 16
7. Plane of the cube and objects based upon it. . " 18
8. Edges from study of the type-solid. . . " 17
9. Corners from study of the type-solid. . . " 17
10. Exercises with sticks and peas. . . . " 18
11. Sewing-cards. . . . . . " 18
12. Tablets laid in borders and groups. . . " 19
13. Stick-laying. . . . . . . " 19
14. Arm and pencil-movements. . . . " 20
15. Draw the square. . . . . . " 20–21
16. Paper-foldings with sewing, stick-laying and drawing. First series, (omitting triangles.) " 22
17. Draw outlines of one view of cubical objects. " 36
18. Paper-folding and cutting, — basket, sled, etc. " 32
19. Paper-folding and pasting. (Designs.) . . " 35
20. Clay plaques. . . . . . " 37

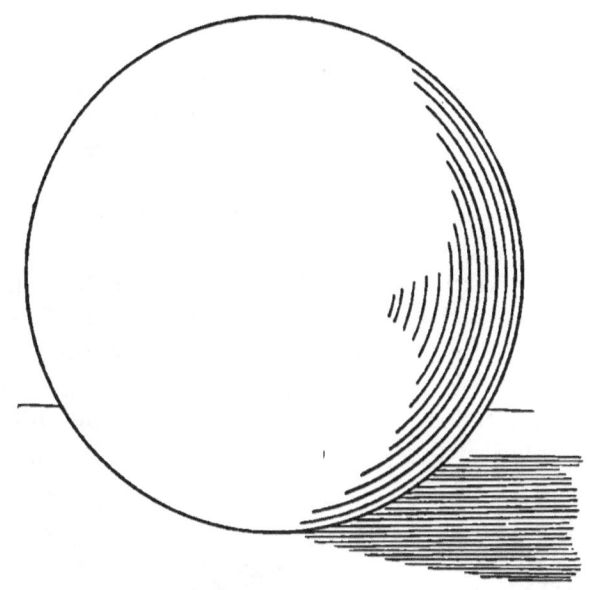

## THE SPHERE.

Each child should hold in his hand a small sphere — while the teacher holds a large one before the class.

The teacher should lead the children to perceive and state that the "ball" is round and smooth, and that it will stand and roll.

Give the name — *sphere*. (Care should be taken that the children do not call this word, *spear*).

Talk about the *outside* of the sphere, and of other objects, and give the name — *surface*.

Let the children move their fingers over the surface of the sphere, and roll the sphere in their hands, and so call forth the expression — *round surface*.

## THE SPHERE.

The children may next model a *sphere* of *clay*. Give to each child a piece of clay, a little larger than a cubic inch, and tell him to place it in the palm of his left hand. Then place the palm of his right hand upon the clay, and roll it and mould it, till a sphere has been formed. The teacher should model one at the same time, that the children may observe the process.

Next, place before the class objects based upon the sphere — as, an apple, a round melon, and a round basket. (Figs. 1 — 3).

Let the children model a sphere, and then change the form of its surface to resemble the object selected. This attempt to imitate in clay, trains both the eye and hand, and will lead the

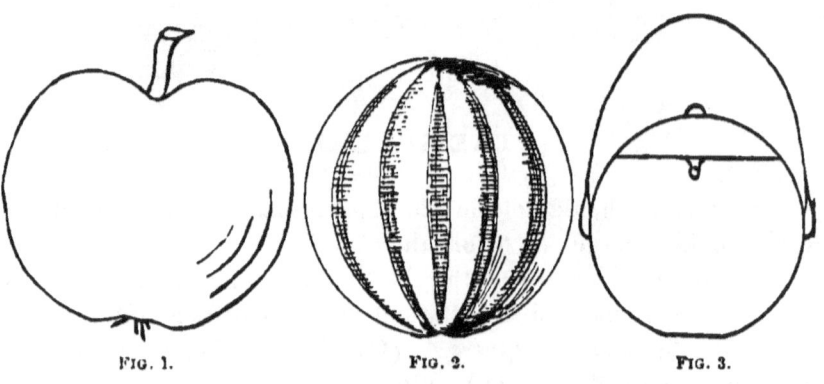

FIG. 1.   FIG. 2.   FIG. 3.

children to notice the spherical form of other objects. To make an apple, the sphere must be indented by pressing slightly with the thumb upon the surface, and then inserting a stem, which may be made of clay, though a real apple stem would prove more

## THE SPHERE.

effective. On the side opposite the stem make a few scratches on the clay, to imitate the blossom. (Fig. 1).

A melon is made by flattening the upper and lower surface a trifle, and marking the stripes. For this, use a sharp slate pencil, a wooden tooth-pick, or a thin strip of wood shaped like a knife-blade.

The basket should have a line marked around it, to represent the edge of the cover. Roll a small piece of clay between the hands, until a long thin strip is made, which may be fastened to the basket for a handle.

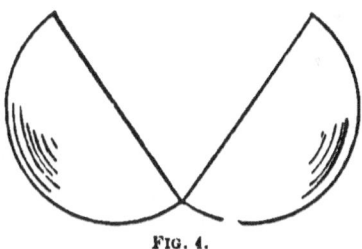

FIG. 4.

A sphere may be cut in halves, and the *hemisphere* described — but it is best to make the study of the hemisphere a separate subject. (Fig. 4).

TABLETS.—Work with *tablets* should follow clay modelling. Place square and circular tablets, (thin card-board) of the same diameter as the type-solids, upon a table where the children can see them.

Tell the children to hold the sphere in front of the eye, and then ask a child to select a tablet that looks like a picture of the sphere.

THE SPHERE.

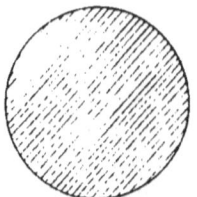

Give the name of the tablet — *circle*.

Let the children place the tablets upon the desk in a position to imitate spherical objects — as a string of beads, or a bunch of grapes. (Figs. 5 and 6).

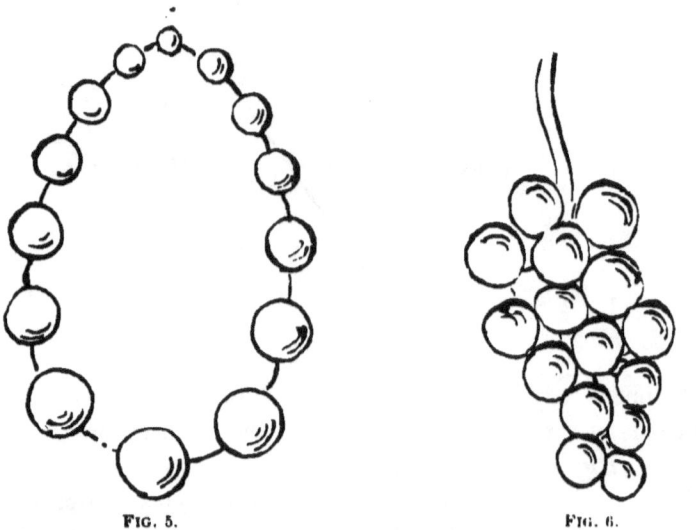

FIG. 5.   FIG. 6.

With colored circles of various sizes very pleasing pictures of objects can be easily made, and the children should be taught to paste the tablets upon gray, or other neutral-tinted paper.

## THE SPHERE.

The spherical outline may also be taught by *sewing cards* having circles or circular objects pricked upon them. Let the children sew with appropriate colored worsteds or threads.

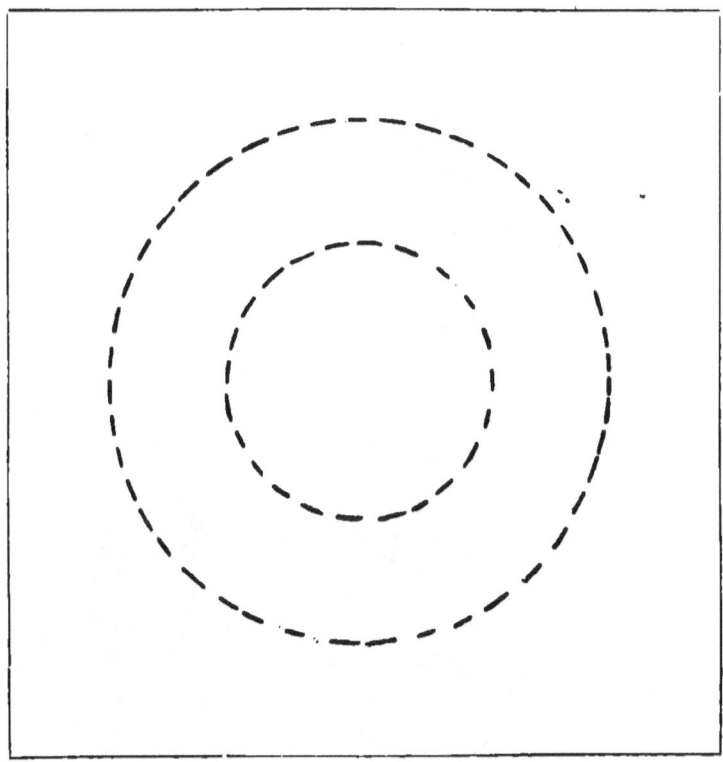

SAMPLE OF SEWING CARD.

# THE SPHERE.

SUBJECTS FOR SEWING CARDS.

## ARM AND PENCIL-MOVEMENT.

The children should next be taught arm and pencil-movements, preparatory to drawing the circle.

Let the children extend the right arm horizontally, and describe the form of the circle in the air, by moving the hand toward the left side, then up — then down toward the right side, and back to point of starting.

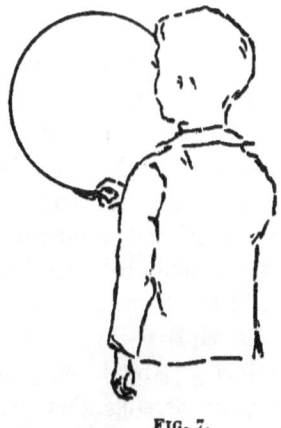

FIG. 7.

Let them practice the same movement at the black-board, using the chalk, until a smooth, free circular movement of the arm is obtained, without regard to the size of the circle, except that it be a large one. The chalk should be held with the pointed end at an angle of about forty-five degrees to the surface of the board, always pointing toward the left, and the circle drawn as indicated by figure.

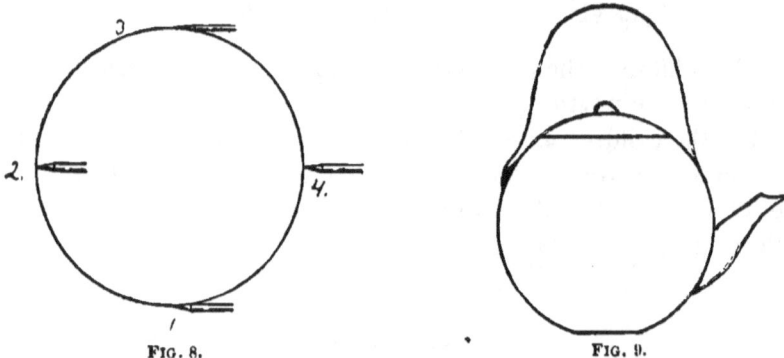

FIG. 8.    FIG. 9.

Let the children practise upon slate or paper, (paper is preferable) holding the pencil in the same manner as the chalk.

Children should draw simple spherical forms *from the object*. Their attention should be called to the prominent features of the object selected. If it is not perfectly round, ask them where the surface is flat or elevated; whether it is longer "one way than the other," also what additions are made to the spherical form to complete the object? Train the child to *see* the form — and afterward, orally, and by drawing, to give descriptive explanations.

Suppose the object selected to be drawn was a *spherical tea-kettle*.

The children will find, by measuring, that the body of the kettle is longer horizontally than vertically. That the distance from the top of the kettle to the highest curve of the handle is equal to one-half the diameter of the circle. They will also discover that the bottom of the kettle and the edge of the cover *look straight*, and that the spout is placed nearer the lower, than the upper part of the *right* side of the kettle. (Fig. 9).

# THE CUBE.

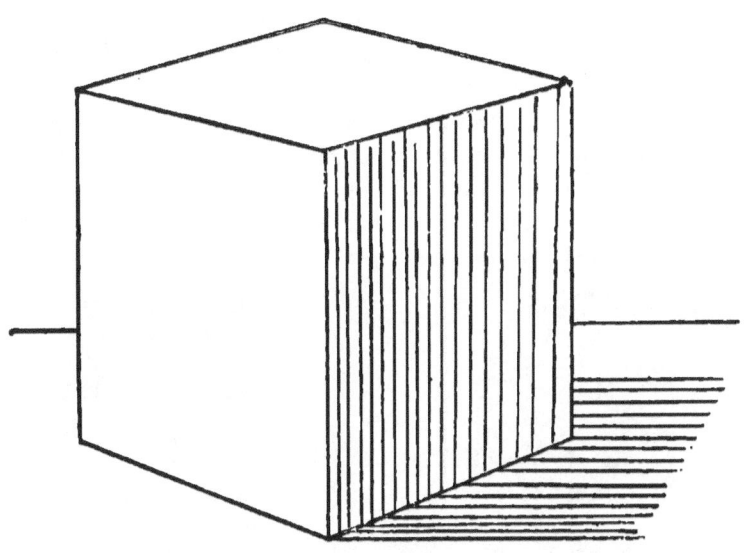

## THE CUBE.

In the study of the *cube*, use type solids as with the sphere.

Compare the cube with the sphere.

Observe that the cube is not round, that it has edges and corners, that it will stand and slide, but will not roll.

Observe also that its surface is flat or plane. There are six parts to the outside of the "*block*," all parts of the same size and shape.

Give the name — *cube*.

When the children have become familiar with the *facts* of the *type solid*, they should be taught to mould the *cube of clay*.

## THE CUBE.

Give a piece of clay to each child, and have them all model a sphere. Then holding the sphere in the right hand, between the thumb and fingers, tap it gently upon the slate three times (the teacher counting aloud for this movement, that the action may be uniform).

Turn the clay and tap three times upon the opposite side, continuing to turn the clay until the *six sides* have been flattened, and the clay has assumed the form of the cube.

Direct the children to be careful to make all the *faces* of the same size, with *sharp edges* and *square corners*.

FIG. 1.

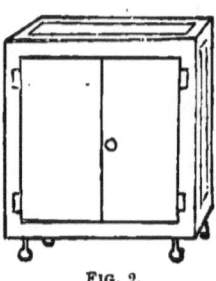

FIG. 2.

Objects like the cube, as a square basket, a safe, dice, lump of sugar, may also be modeled in clay. (Figs. 1 and 2).

The *cube* should also be formed of *paper*.

Give each child a square of paper. The teacher holds a *large square* before the class, and folds and dictates; while the children follow her directions.

Fold front edge to meet back edge. Open paper. Fold front edge to meet centre fold. Open paper. Fold back edge to meet centre fold. Open. Fold left edge to meet right edge. Open. Fold left edge to meet centre fold. Open. Fold right edge to meet centre. Open. Result,— sixteen small squares.

## THE CUBE.

Cut off one entire row of squares from the lower side of paper. From the larger piece cut off each corner square. The paper now is like **Fig. 1**.

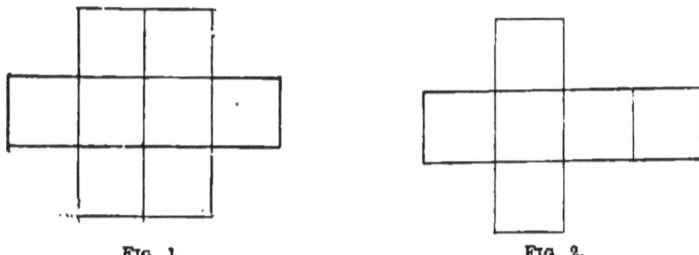

FIG. 1.  FIG. 2.

Now, cut off one of the two upper squares and also the one opposite on the lower row. (Fig. 2).

Fold this paper till the edges meet in the form of a cube — join the edges by sewing or pasting.

Many objects, based upon the cube, may be made of paper.

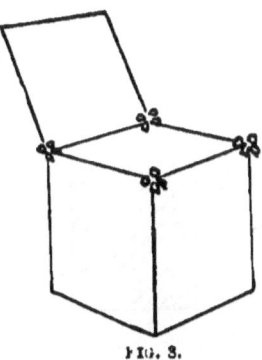

FIG. 3.

By joining (as for the cube) all the faces, except one, a box is formed. The face left open serves for the cover. Instead of sewing the edges, tie each corner with colored worsted. (Fig. 3).

## FACE OF THE CUBE.

Let the children find and count the different parts of the surface of the cube.

There are six parts — all of the same size.

Each part is called a *face*. Find the front face — top face — and the other faces.

Give exercises that will illustrate the terms — *level* and *upright*.

Let the children find surfaces, upon which objects will rest evenly.

Give term — *horizontal*.

Find the horizontal faces of the cube.

Let the children place object in upright position.

Find the faces of cube that are upright.

Give term — *vertical*.

Find a *tablet* like one face of the cube.

Give name — *square*.

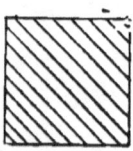

Find horizontal and vertical faces.

Interesting and valuable exercises with tablets may be given.

FACE OF THE CUBE. 17

Place six tablets to form a cube, like the paper model of the cube.

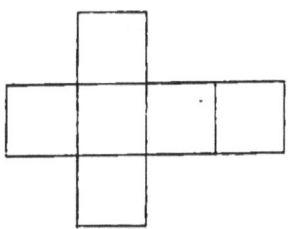

EDGES.— Direct the children to find the places on the cube, and on different objects about the room, where the *faces meet*.

Give term — *edge*.

Find horizontal and vertical edges.

Find any *two* edges of the *cube* that extend in the same direction—for example, those from left to right, also those from front to back, and again those from top to bottom. And give the term — *parallel*.

CORNERS. Have the children find the points where the edges meet, and give the name — *corner*.

Have them find also, the *outside corners* of the cube — and of other objects.

Also find the inside corners of the room, and of boxes — find *face* corners of the *cube*, of the *floor* and of the *slates*.

A skeleton cube can also be formed of *sticks and peas* by

## FACE OF THE CUBE.

placing the sticks to represent the edges of the cube, and joining the corners with peas.

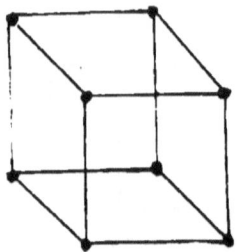

Cut a plane from a clay cube and from it model a square cracker, or a card of buttons.

Square objects may be outlined on sewing cards, and given the children to sew.

## FACE OF THE CUBE.

Make borders of tablets using both squares and circles — edge to edge.

Next, place them with their edges near, but not touching.

Edges overlapping.

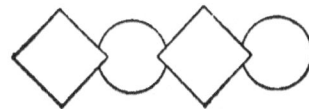

In groups.

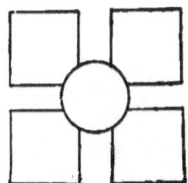

Lay sticks for edges to the borders.

Tablets of colored paper pasted on coarse paper make pretty borders.

STICK LAYING.— Lay sticks to represent the edges and corners of a square.

## ARM AND PENCIL-MOVEMENT.

The next step is to give arm and pencil-movements preparatory to drawing the square. Send as many children as possible to the board —the others meanwhile working at their desks.

Direct the children to turn slightly toward the left, and hold the point of the chalk toward the left also, at an angle of forty-five degrees to the surface of the board — draw downward in a vertical line. (Fig. 1).

FIG. 1.

Now, direct the children at the board to turn slightly toward the right, and with the chalk pointing upward, place the point at the upper end of the vertical line, and draw from left to right, a line as long as the vertical line. (Fig. 2).

# ARM AND PENCIL-MOVEMENT.

FIG. 2.

Turn again toward the left — and draw downward from the right end of the horizontal line, to make the right vertical line. Resume position for the horizontal line, and draw the lower side of the square, from left to right. (Fig. 3).

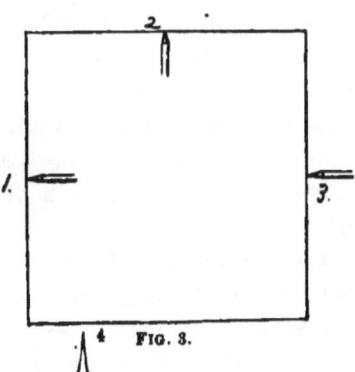

FIG. 3.

In drawing on the black-board the children may use a ruler to measure the lines but must not draw by it.

## PAPER-FOLDING.

The following foldings form a systematic series, but some of them, for example, the angles and triangles, may be omitted until after the study of the solids illustrating those forms. These foldings may be used separately, but it is well to connect them with drawing and sewing lessons. Thus after folding No. 1, fold another just like it and let the child trace the crease with a lead pencil. Next with a ruler measure the line and draw one the same length on slate or paper, testing carefully with ruler. In this way the use of ruler is learned, and eye and hand trained to accuracy. Then draw the line again entirely free-hand.

These four steps having been taken, a child will thoroughly understand and be able to draw a horizontal line.

Proceed the same with No. 2, and all the figures, taking four steps with each before attempting the next figure.

These same figures can be pricked on cards and sewed with colored thread or worsted, giving a series of sewing lessons.

Sewing on canvas or scrim will do as well.

If the papers are cut through the creases and the strips pasted on gray or neutral-tinted coarse paper, another development of manual training will result.

Stick-laying in these forms should precede drawing.

The papers used for these foldings are four inches square.

In this first set of foldings each crease should be made separately that all may be accurate. Never allow the children to double the paper and make several creases at once.

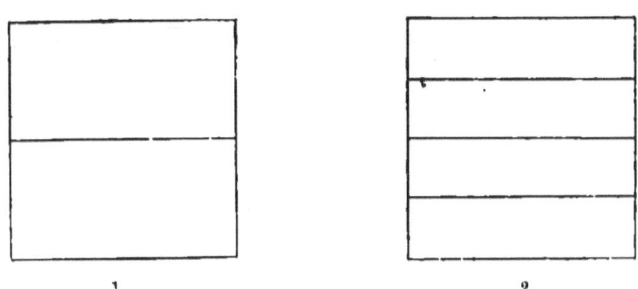

1.   2.

NUMBER ONE. —Fold front edge of square to meet back edge. Open paper. Result — a horizontal line.

NUMBER TWO. —Fold front edge of square to meet back edge. Open paper. Fold front edge to meet horizontal line in centre. Fold back edge to meet centre line. Open square. Result — three parallel horizontal lines.

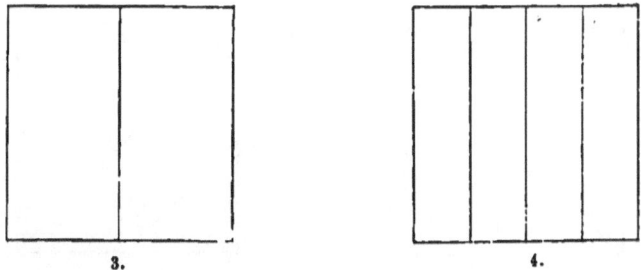

3.   4.

NUMBER THREE. — Fold left edge to meet right edge. Open paper. Result — vertical line.

NUMBER FOUR. — Fold left edge to meet right edge. Open paper. Fold left edge to meet centre line. Fold right edge to meet centre line. Result — three parallel vertical lines.

PAPER-FOLDING.

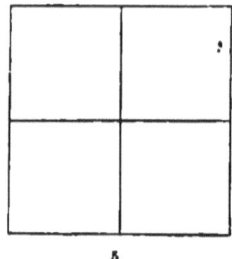

5.

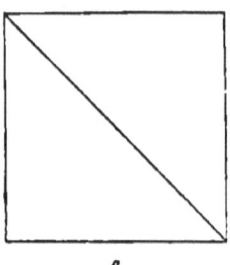

6.

NUMBER FIVE. — Fold front edge to meet back edge. Open paper. Fold left edge to meet right edge. Open paper. Result — two diameters of square.

NUMBER SIX. — Fold lower left corner of square to meet upper right corner. Open paper. Result — oblique line — also diagonal of square.

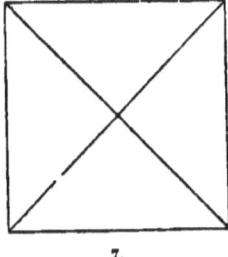

7.

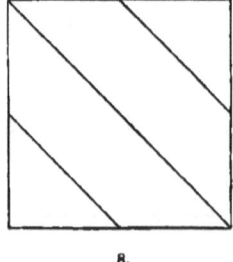

8.

NUMBER SEVEN. — Fold lower left corner to meet upper right corner. Open paper. Fold lower right corner to meet upper left corner. Open paper. Result — two diagonals of square.

PAPER-FOLDING.                               25

NUMBER EIGHT.— Fold lower left corner of square to meet upper right corner. Open paper. Fold lower left corner to meet centre of oblique line. Fold upper right corner to meet centre line. Open paper. Result — three parallel oblique lines.

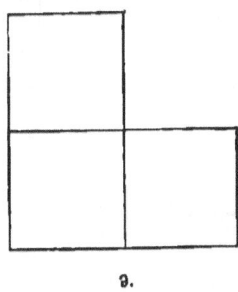

9.

NUMBER NINE. — Fold diameters of square (See No. 5). Result — four small squares. Cut out upper right square. Result — right angle.

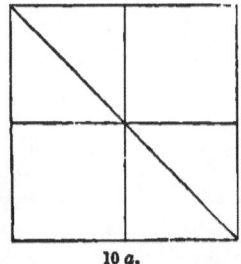
10 a.

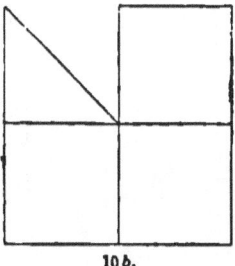
10 b.

NUMBER TEN.—Fold diameters of square. Open square. Fold lower left corner to meet upper right corner. Open paper. (No. 10 a).

Cut out triangle in upper left square. Result — acute angle. (No. 10 b).

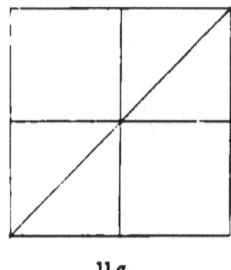
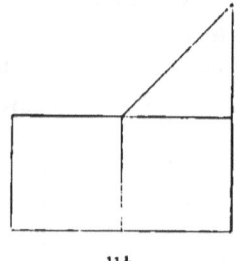

11 a.　　　　　　　　　11 b.

NUMBER ELEVEN. — Fold diameters of square. Open paper. Fold lower right corner to meet upper left corner. Open paper. (No. 11 a). Cut out upper left square and adjoining triangle. Result — obtuse angle. (No. 11 b).

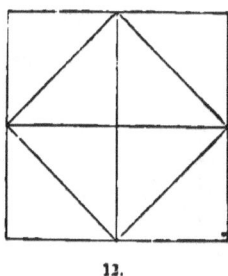

12.

NUMBER TWELVE. — Fold diameters of square. Open paper. Fold each corner of square to centre of square. Open paper. Result — inscribed square.

PAPER-FOLDING. 27

NUMBER THIRTEEN. — Hold right edge of square in right hand and left edge in left hand. Pass right hand under towards left, and left over towards right till upper side of square is divided into thirds. (See No. 13 a). When the upper edge is lapped so it is even at both ends press the creases down the whole length of paper. Open paper. Result — square divided vertically into thirds. (No. 13 b).

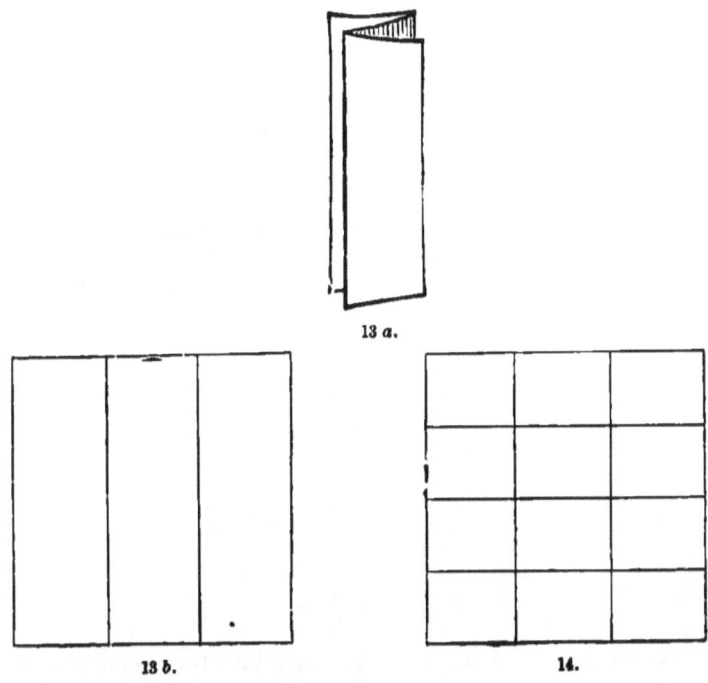

NUMBER FOURTEEN. — Fold square in three horizontal, parallel lines. (See No. 2). Open paper. Fold upper side into thirds. (See No. 13 a). Open paper. Result — three parallel horizontal lines divided into thirds.

NUMBER FIFTEEN.—Fold left side of square so it will be divided into thirds as No. 13 *a*. Press paper in two horizontal folds. Open paper. Result — square divided into thirds horizontally.

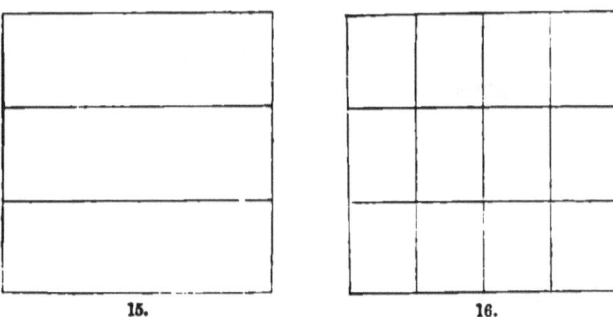

15.    16.

NUMBER SIXTEEN.— Fold square into three parallel vertical lines. (See No. 4.) Open paper. Divide into thirds. (See No. 15.) Open paper. Result—three parallel, vertical lines divided into thirds.

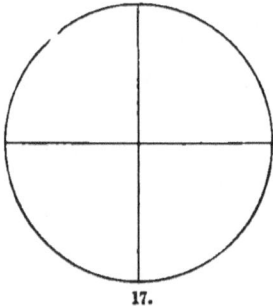

17.

NUMBER SEVENTEEN. — Fold square into four small squares by folding front edge to meet back edge. Then left edge of oblong to meet right edge. Hold corner which forms the centre of the paper in left hand. Cut in a line curving outward from lower right corner of square to upper left corner. Open paper. Result — circle.

PAPER-FOLDING. 29

NUMBER EIGHTEEN.—Cut a circle. (See No. 17). Cut through one diameter. Result—semi-circle..

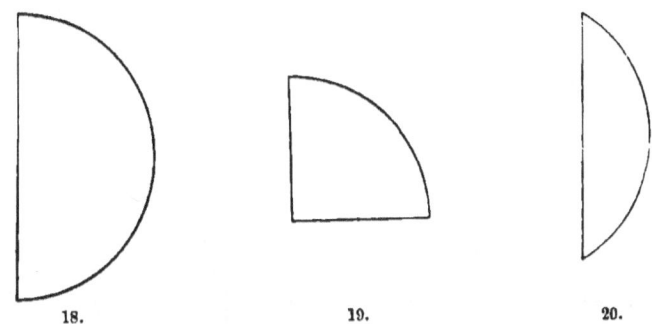

18.   19.   20.

NUMBER NINETEEN. — Cut circle. (See No. 17). Cut from edge of circle through half of horizontal diameter — also from centre of circle through one half vertical diameter. Quarter circle.

NUMBER TWENTY. — Cut circle. (See No. 17). Fold edge at end of one diameter to meet centre of same diameter. Open paper. Cut off small section. Result — curved edge or small section of circle.

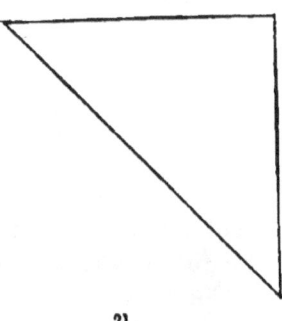

21.

NUMBER TWENTY-ONE. — Fold lower left corner to meet upper-right corner. Cut through diagonal. Result — right-angled triangle.

30  PAPER-FOLDING.

NUMBER TWENTY-TWO. — Fold front edge to meet back edge. Open paper. Fold front edge to meet centre fold. Open paper. Fold back edge to meet centre fold. Open. Fold left edge to meet

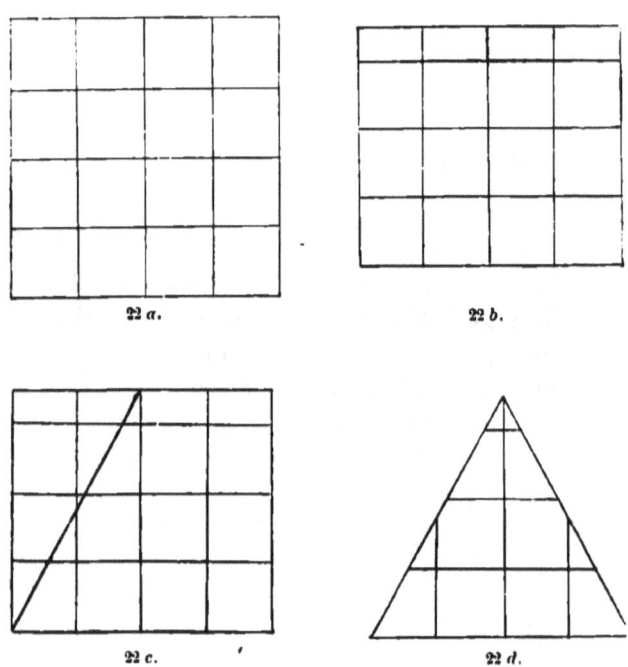

right edge. Open. Fold left edge to meet centre vertical fold. Open. Fold right edge to meet centre fold. Open. Result — sixteen small squares. (No. 22 a.) Cut off from entire upper side of square a strip equal to one-eighth the width of square or one-half-inch. (No. 22 b). Fold back upper left corner of paper so that the

PAPER-FOLDING.                                31

crease will extend from upper end of vertical diameter to lower left corner of paper. (No. 22 c). Fold back upper right corner so the crease will extend from upper end of vertical diameter to lower right corner of paper. Cut through the last two folds. Result — equilateral triangle. (No. 22 d).

NUMBER TWENTY-THREE. — Fold lower left corner so crease extends from upper left corner to middle of lower side of square. Cut through fold. Result — the smaller section is a scalene triangle.

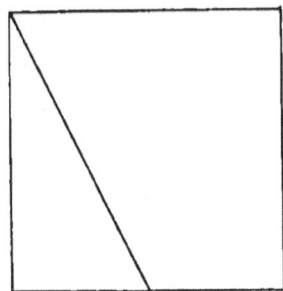 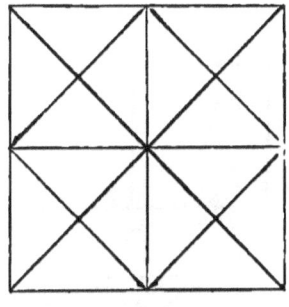

24.

NUMBER TWENTY-FOUR. — Fold square in four small squares. (See first part of No. 17). Fold again to get diagonals of small square. Open paper. Result — four squares with diagonals forming construction lines for various designs.

## PAPER-FOLDING ILLUSTRATING OBJECTS BASED UPON SOLIDS.

As the square is the form from which the greatest variety of paper-folding and design can be obtained, it can be used throughout the course interspersed with studies from all the type-solids.

Many of the Kindergarten forms can be used with advantage. Here is a simple one, a little basket.

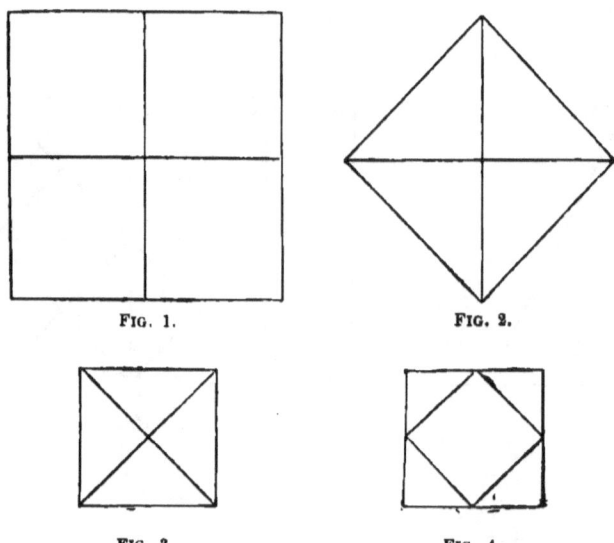

FIG. 1.　　FIG. 2.

FIG. 3.　　FIG. 4.

NUMBER ONE. — Fold front edge of square to meet back edge. Open. Fold left edge to meet right edge. Open. (Fig. 1). Fold each corner to centre of square, (Fig. 2). Turn paper. Fold each corner to centre, (Fig. 3). Turn paper. Fold back each of the corners that meet in the centre, (Fig. 4). Insert the fingers and thumb in the pockets thus made and press the four under corners together. Result — Fig. 5.

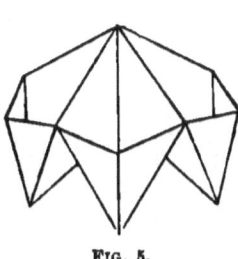

FIG. 5.

NUMBER TWO. — Fold front edge of square to meet back edge. Open. Fold front edge to meet centre fold. Fold back edge to meet centre.

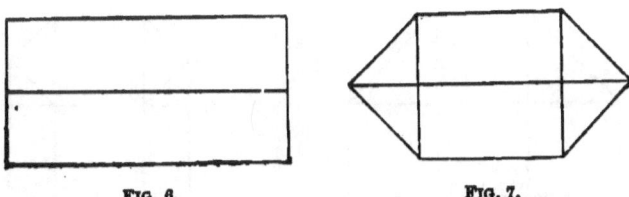

FIG. 6.    FIG. 7.

Turn paper — longest edges horizontal. Fold upper and lower left corners to meet on horizontal line. Fold right corners the same way. (Fig. 7).

PAPER-FOLDING.

Fold upper edge to meet lower edge. (Fig. 8). Result — a boat. (Fig. 9).

FIG. 8.   FIG. 9.

NUMBER THREE. — Divide (by folding) a square into thirds, both vertically and horizontally. (Fig. 10).

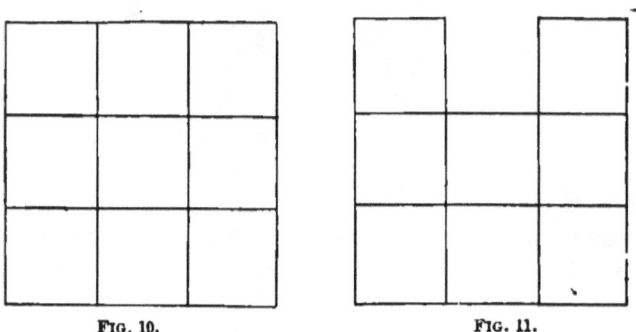

FIG. 10.   FIG. 11.

Cut out the middle square on upper side. (Fig. 11).

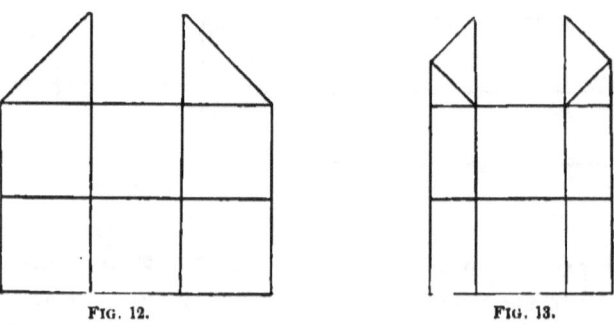

FIG. 12.   FIG. 13.

## PAPER-FOLDING.

Fold upper right corner of upper right square to meet the lower left corner of same square. Fold upper left corner of upper left square to meet the opposite corner of the same square. (Fig. 12).

Fold right edge of paper to meet the vertical crease next it. Fold left edge of square to meet vertical crease next it. (Fig. 13). Turn paper. Result — a sled. (Fig. 14).

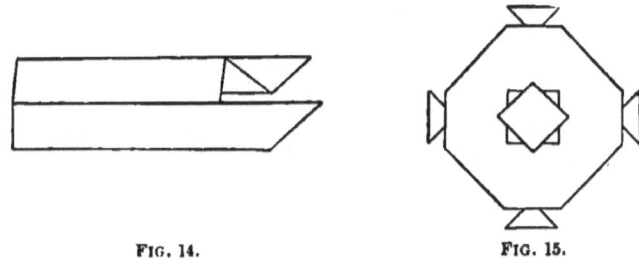

FIG. 14.     FIG. 15.

NUMBER FOUR. — Let the children cut Kindergarten designs from colored paper and paste upon gray square.

The following is easily made. Fold front edge to meet back edge. Fold left edge to meet right edge. Fold lower left corner to meet upper right corner. Open. Fold lower left corner to meet centre of square. Fold upper right corner to meet centre of square. Cut off both corners through the folds last made. Open the large figure and paste on gray square. Open the corner cut from lower left corner of square. It is a little square. Paste diagonally across open centre of the octagonal figure. The other corners cut off are triangles. Paste them around four sides of large figure. (Fig. 15).

During the lesson each child can have a little plate of paste, and wooden tooth-picks are better than brushes with which to apply the paste.

VIEWS OF CUBICAL OBJECTS.

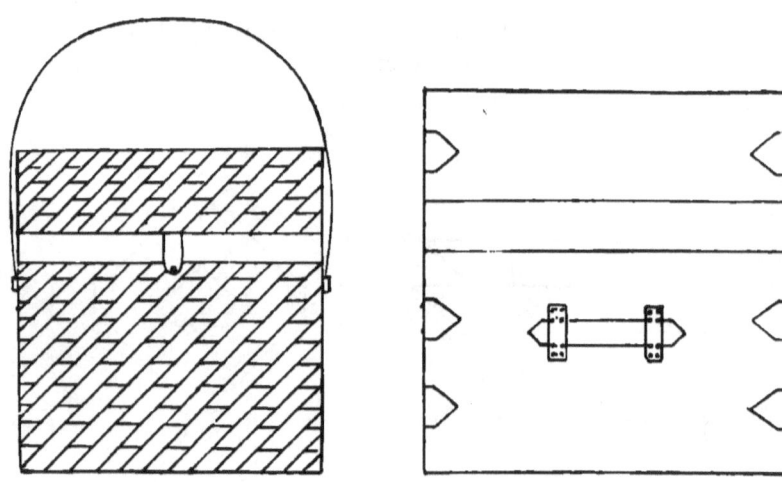

## DRAWING THE VIEWS OF CUBICAL OBJECTS.

Drawing from cubical objects should be practiced as with the sphere. The objects which have been modeled in clay, and also *cubical objects* in the room should be drawn. At first, it is best to draw views of each *face* separately, as young children are rarely able to draw correctly, when views involving perspective are attempted.

Cubical boxes, and baskets, toy money-banks, toy trunks, (see illustration) and similar objects are suitable subjects.

Another step in clay work may follow the paper-folding and drawing.

Cut from a large cube a plane about one-quarter inch in thickness or make a square tablet by placing bits of clay on a slate and moulding them into a flat smooth surface.

With a sharp slate pencil, draw simple designs upon the clay. Clay can be added within the outline of the figure, building it up in bas-relief if desired, or if left in flat outline a pretty effect will be given by puncturing the surface of the clay around the design.

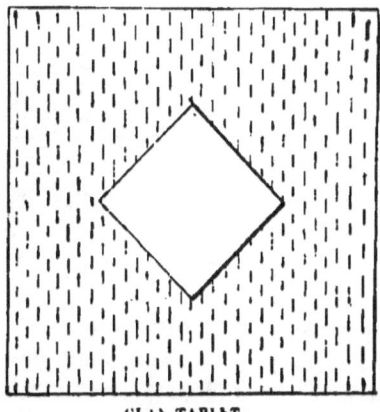
CLAY TABLET.

Nearly all the figures used in the drawing course can be repeated upon clay. The youngest pupils can have various plane figures cut from card-board, and placing them on the clay, *trace* around the edges.

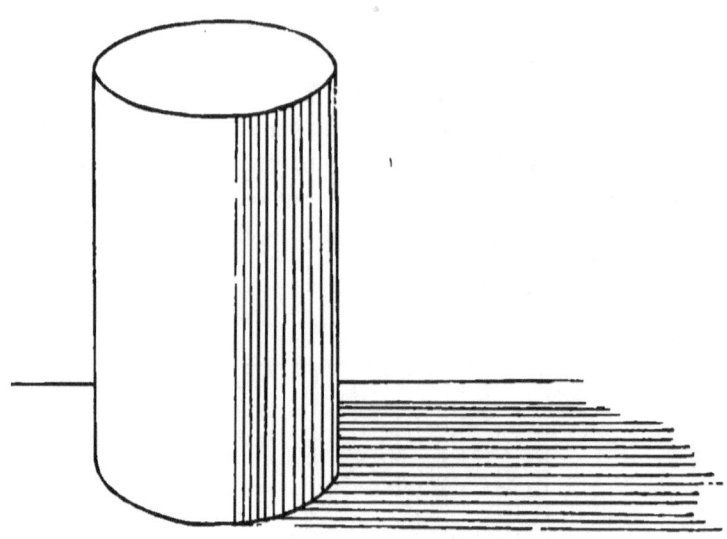

## THE CYLINDER.

Use the *type-solids* as in the previous lessons. Direct the children to compare the *cylinder*, with the *sphere*, and the *cube*. They will discover that it will roll, and stand, and that its surface is plane and curved. The *plane faces* are *circles*. Give the name — *cylinder*.

The children can model a cylinder of clay, by first making a sphere, and then rolling it on a slate, or, between the hands, until the desired length is obtained. Then flatten the ends by tapping them alternately upon the slate.

THE CYLINDER. 39

Cylindrical objects can now be made of clay, as, a rolling-pin, muff, water-pot, drum, and bottle.

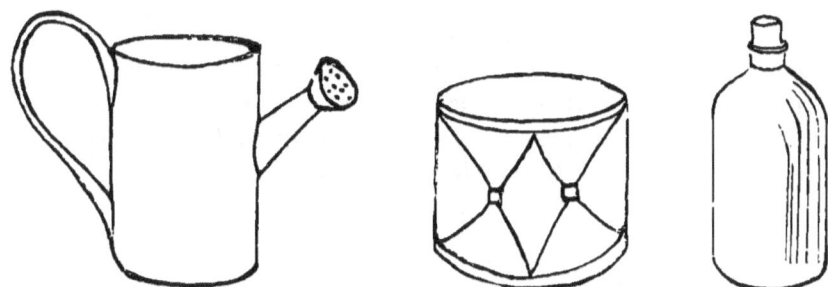

For a *rolling-pin*, make a cylinder of the desired length. Then make *small* cylinders for handles; *instead of flattening* the outer ends of the handles, *curve* them slightly.

The rolling-pin and the handles may be joined together more firmly, by inserting in the *joined ends* a wooden tooth-pick. Join spouts to tea-kettles and watering pots in the same manner.

A *paper cylinder* may next be made.

Fold a square into sixteen small squares. Cut out each corner square, and all of the two lower squares, except a slight margin as in Fig. 1.

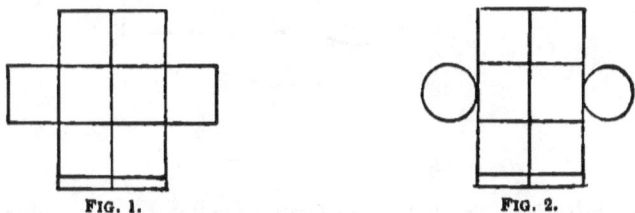

FIG. 1.   FIG. 2.

Cut circles from the squares on left and right sides, leaving the circles attached to the paper. (Fig. 2).

Fasten the upper and lower edges of paper together by sewing or pasting, and join the circles to the ends of the hollow cylinder thus formed.

Make another *clay cylinder*, and cut it in halves, through its longest diameter. Scoop out a portion of the clay from a *half-cylinder*, and a trough is made. By attaching the trough to an upright cylinder the principal parts of a pump are formed. To complete the pump, add the handle and spout.

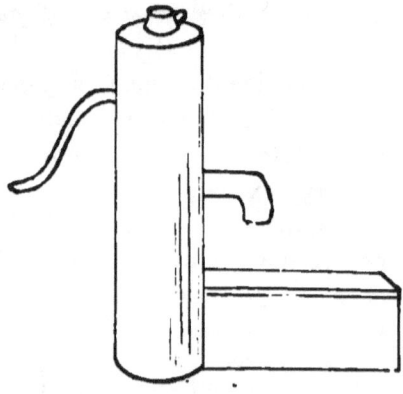

The *half-cylinder*, may also form a basket by the addition of a handle.

## THE CYLINDER.

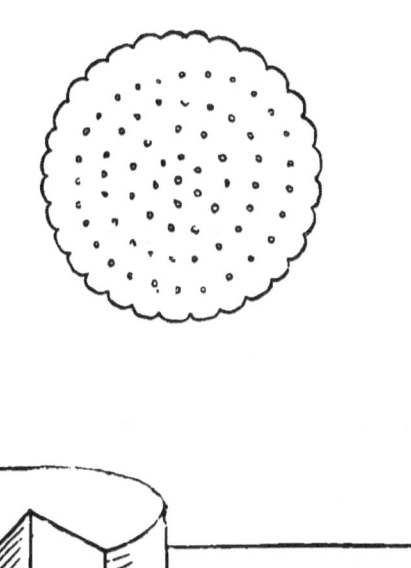

Cut a thin slice from the end of a cylinder and mould it into a round cracker.

From a *thicker slice* may be moulded a cheese, or a circular box.

## THE CYLINDER.

Let the children hold a cylinder in a vertical position, in front of the eye and study the outline.

Then find a tablet like it.

Give the name — *oblong*.

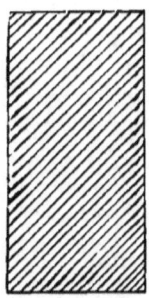

Let the children find tablets like the upper and lower *faces* of the cylinders—(circles).

All these tablets may be arranged in groups.

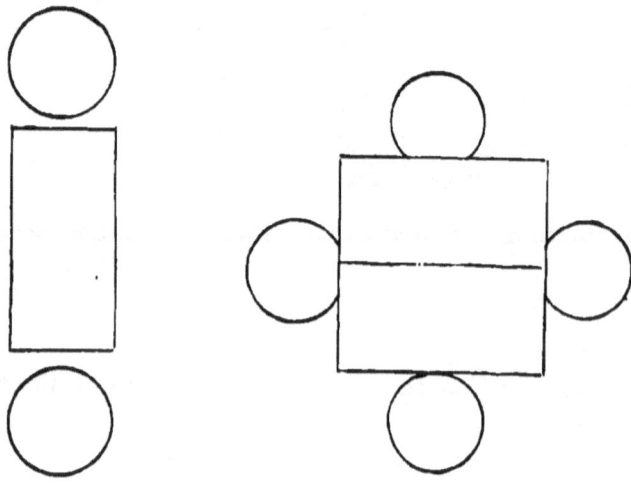

## THE CYLINDER.

Ask the children to cut an *oblong plane* and a *circular plane*, from the *clay cylinder*. Figures containing oblongs may be traced on clay plaques, or sewed on cards.

A great variety of forms, *combining oblongs, squares* and *circles* may now be introduced.

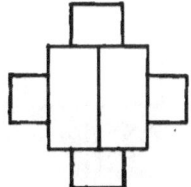 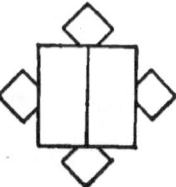

The *oblong* can be made easily, by cutting a square in halves. Oblongs of other proportions should also be introduced at this stage.

## THE CYLINDER.

Fold a square to mark its diameters, and then use the entire length, and various portions of the width, for different sized oblongs.

Fold another paper and using the creases for diameters, draw the outline of an oblong.

Lay *sticks* to form the outline of the *oblong*.

Give arm and pencil-movements as for a square, and draw the oblong.

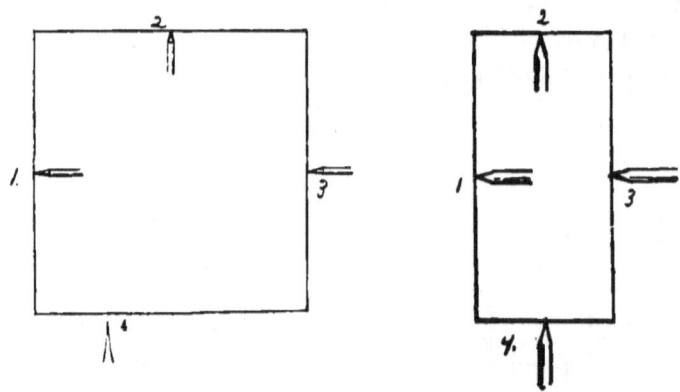

Draw from *objects, cylindrical forms* and have the children describe each object in a language lesson.

## REVIEW OF SOLIDS.

Direct the children to FEEL of the sphere — cube — cylinder — and from the sense of *touch alone*, describe these solids.

Then, a child may describe to the class, one of the solids (*without showing it*) and the class be asked to name the solid thus described.

The faces of solids may be reviewed in the same manner.

---

## VIEWS OF SOLIDS.

Tell the children to place a sphere upon their desks and *look down* upon it. This view of the sphere is called a *top view* and when *drawn*, is represented by a circle. Direct the children to draw the *top view*.

Then ask the children to hold the sphere on a level with the eye. This view is called the *front view*. Let the children draw this *front* view and the result will be a *circle*, as before.

Then hold sphere *above the eye* — this view is called the bottom view. Draw it and obtain another circle.

Place the cube and cylinder in *similar positions* and draw the views.

*Build up* a group of these solids and draw the front view.

The teacher should frequently describe to her class these solids, (without showing them) and direct the children to draw the solids thus described.

## COLOR.

The study of color should now be introduced. As color holds a prominent position in educational progress, knowledge of the best methods of teaching it becomes essential. That the correct blending of color is but little understood, is clearly evinced in our daily surroundings, and the wisdom of introducing to our youngest pupils even, a practical course of instruction in harmony of color is beyond question.

Many publications upon the subject deal largely with the theory of color as applied to painting. The use of the brush is one method of illustrating color, but there are other methods more practicable for general work in large classes of young children.

Some suggestions of methods to be avoided and of others that have proved successful in primary classes may prove helpful.

Care should be taken to avoid teaching *terms* only, instead of giving material object lessons. Many teachers devote much time to engraving upon the minds of their pupils the *names* of primary and secondary colors.

While it may be, as claimed by some scientists, that red, green and violet are primary in accordance with the vibration of certain optic nerves — still, red, yellow and blue *pigments* are primary as they form the basis of other combinations.

Yet it is not necessary to burden the *children's* minds with this.

Care also should be taken when presenting the subject of *complementary colors*, to eradicate that deplorable taste that delights in such combinations as flaming orange with brightest blue, lest a repetition of the case occur, where the little girl insisted upon dressing her dolls in those outré colors because her teacher used them in paper designs and taught her to combine them.

The great object to be sought is the proper use or harmony of color. Nature should be our model. Children must first learn color by sight and name through association with color. The rainbow is pure color, and the colors which more nearly resemble it are called standard colors; for example, carmine is a standard red.

For the first lesson suspend before the class a large piece of standard red paper, and one of standard yellow.

Have a half-pint bottle nearly full of water and dissolve a little carmine water-color paint in the bottle till the liquid is of proper color and another pleasing object of standard red is presented.

Do the same with chrome yellow.

Paste paper of these same colors on small cards and distribute among the children.

Let each child match the card to the large paper.

Each child name color of large papers.

Each child find red and yellow cards as called for.

Each child tell name of color of card as given.

Teach blue in the same way. The best blue for the liquid is cobalt. Review the three colors.

Objects made by folding colored papers is one pleasing method of testing the knowledge of children in this review.

To teach orange, hold before the class a clear glass tumbler. Pour into it a little of the red liquid, then an equal quantity of yellow liquid. The mixture is orange, and the transformation taking place before the children's eyes fixes their attention, and the name of the new color, orange, is more easily remembered.

48                                     COLOR.

Suspend a large orange paper, and giving the children orange and yellow cards, let them match, distinguish, and name.

Place yellow tissue-paper upon red tissue paper. Allow the light to shine through, and orange is seen. These papers can be folded into pretty forms.

Gelatine films also illustrate the blending of colors.

A red and a yellow triangle with a square of orange between them may be pasted upon gray paper to illustrate the fact that red and yellow make orange.

Also make them in worsted, on Kindergarten cards.

Teach green by mixing blue and yellow the same as red and yellow. Use paper forms, worsted, and any practical illustration of the subject. Teach violet by mixing red and blue.

This circular diagram will illustrate the relation of colors previously mentioned.

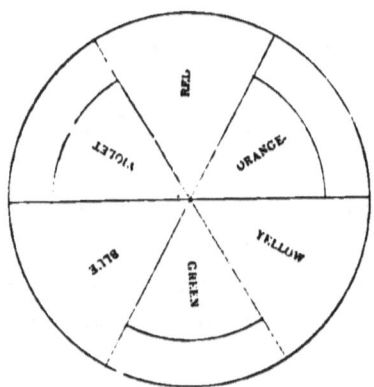

Thus the orange is placed between red and yellow because it is produced by the mixture of those two colors.

For a similar reason green is placed between yellow and blue,—and violet between blue and red.

Let children bring objects of these different colors.

Name colors of objects remembered but not seen in the schoolroom.

Black and white should be noticed, and brown and gray taught.

Colors are pleasing to children, and if they are allowed to *make* something of these pretty papers and worsted, under proper guidance their taste in color will be easily cultivated.

These different standard colors cannot be *combined* in any simple work the children could make at this stage, but any *one* of these bright colors can be used with gray or some other neutral tint.

Tones lighter and darker than the standard should be taught.

Mix the standard red liquid with white, (Chinese white) also with black (India ink).

Describe as light, and dark red. Have papers of several shades of red, but all belonging to the same scale. Let children select all the reds from among other colors.

Let them find and name red, light-red, dark-red. Do the same with all the colors previously studied, omitting the mixing of black liquid with yellow or orange as dark-green will result.

Make a chart having three shades of each of the colors, and let the children match exactly with their small cards.

Simple designs may now be made by combining a tint and shade of any one color. Thus light-red with dark-red — light-green with dark-green. Under careful guidance the children will unconsciously learn theory and harmony of color by constant association of proper colors in their daily exercises.

50  COLOR.

Let children describe colored forms, viz., "This is a red circle." "This is a yellow square." "This figure has a large dark-green square and small light-green triangles."

The following designs may be made of paper:

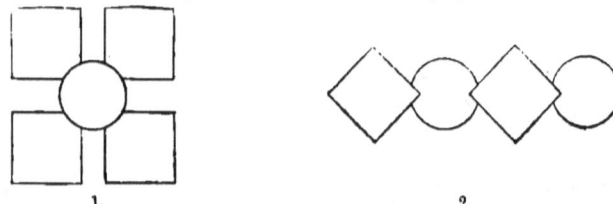

Number One.—Red squares. Black circle.

Number Two.—Yellow circles. Black squares.

Number Three.—Pink circles. Black square.

Number Four.—Large square or two oblongs of dark red, small squares light pink.

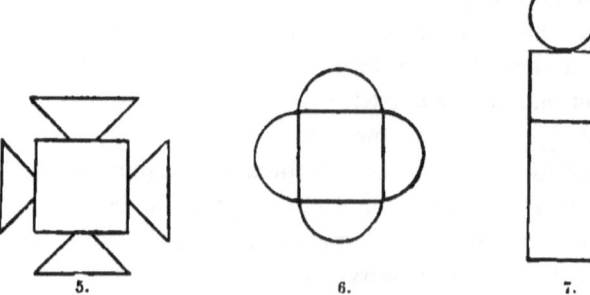

## COLOR.

NUMBER FIVE.—Dark violet square.  Light violet triangles.

NUMBER SIX.—Brown bronze square.  Light, yellow semicircles.

NUMBER SEVEN.—Three shades of one color.

An almost inexhaustible field of color lessons can be found in coloring the clay *forms* made by children.

Dry paint in the form of a powder may be found at the art stores. This powder comes in various shades and tints. If the correct shades of powder be rubbed with the finger upon the clay objects before they harden, the resemblance to the object reproduced will be greatly increased. Treat a clay banana in this way. Cover the clay thoroughly with the correct shade of yellow, and add touches of green on the curves and near the end. A touch of brown on the stem will complete the coloring, and the resemblance to the natural fruit will be quite marked.

The clay peach similarly treated acquires the beautiful velvety appearance characteristic of the fruit.

Children are often perplexed in naming colors by their inability to distinguish a *hue* of color from a *shade* or *tint* of the standard. Thus carmine, scarlet and magenta are all known to them as *red*, but only the carmine can be assigned to the scale of standard red. To explain these differences resort to the colored liquids again. Assuming orange to be produced by mixing equal parts of red and yellow, add more red to the orange and a color is made that may be termed orange-red. By mixing white with orange-red, its tint, (which is salmon) is produced. By mixing black with orange-red, its shade (or scarlet) is produced. These tones are the yellow hues of red.

Show orange again and add more yellow — giving buff or the red hues of yellow. Young children can describe carmine as standard red,— scarlet as a color having more red than yellow — and buff as a color having more yellow than red.

There is one red which has not been mentioned in the scales, but which children are very apt to bring as a sample — viz., magenta. This is a mixture of red and blue like the purple only in unequal quantities, nearly all red with but little blue. The greens can be divided into blue-greens and yellow-greens. For blue-green put more blue than yellow. For yellow-green put more yellow than blue. Violet can be divided the same way. More red than blue, giving red-violet — more blue than red, giving blue-violet.

This chart will be found to illustrate the proper position of the hues of these colors.

| | | HUES. | | HUES. | | HUES. | |
|---|---|---|---|---|---|---|---|
| TINT, | . Pink. | Salmon. | Light Orange. | Buff. | Cream. | Apple Green. | |
| STANDARD, | . Red. | Orange-red. | Orange. | Orange-yellow. | Yellow. | Yellow-green. | |
| SHADE, | . Garnet. | Scarlet. | Dark Orange. | Dark O. Yellow. | Corn. | Dark Y. Green. | |

| | | HUES. | | HUES. | | HUES. | |
|---|---|---|---|---|---|---|---|
| TINT, | . Light Green. | Light-blue Green. | Light Blue. | Lavender. | Light Violet. | Lilac. | |
| STANDARD, | . Green. | Blue-green. | Blue. | Blue Violet. | Violet. | Red Violet. | |
| SHADE, | . Dark Green. | Dark B. Green. | Dark Blue. | Dark B. Violet. | Dark Violet. | Dark R. Violet. | |

## PAPER CUTTING.—COLOR WORK.

The following designs can be cut from paper and placed upon a suitable background allowing the under color to show through the openings. Cut the design from any bright color and place over black, or gray, or white paper. Another set can be made by cutting from a tint and placing over a shade of the same color. If the designs are cut from gold or silver paper and placed over proper colors the effect is agreeable.

Fold the front edge of a square to meet back edge. Fold left edge of oblong to meet right edge. Fold lower right corner to meet upper left corner. Upon the triangle thus formed draw the figures indicated by dotted lines and cut through dotted lines, thus —

Figure A. when opened gives Fig. 1.

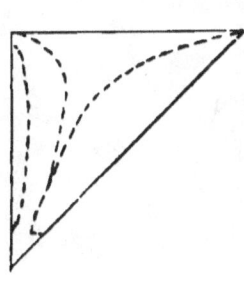

FIG. A.

FIG. 1.

## PAPER-CUTTING.

Figure B. when opened gives Fig. 2.

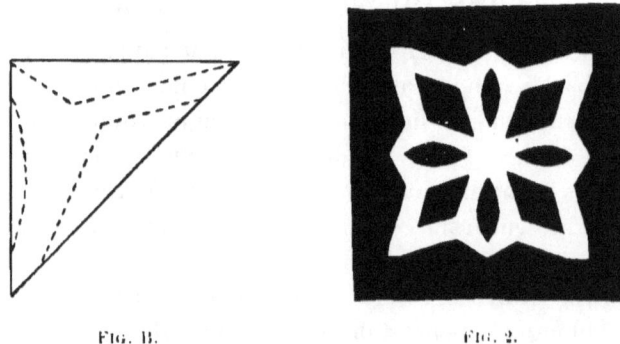

FIG. B.    FIG. 2.

Figure C. when opened gives Fig. 3.

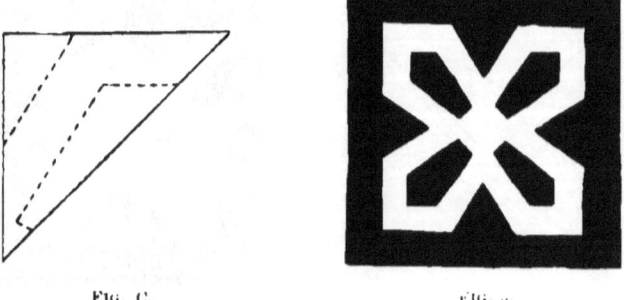

FIG. C.    FIG. 3.

Figure D. when opened gives Fig. 4.

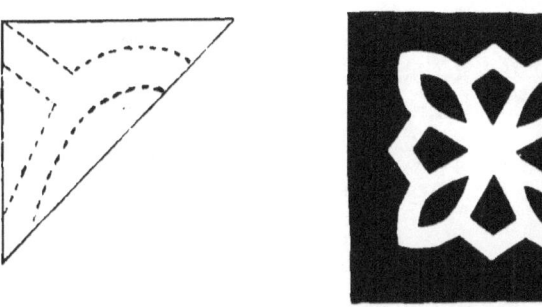

FIG. D.  FIG. 4.

Figure E. when opened gives Fig. 5.

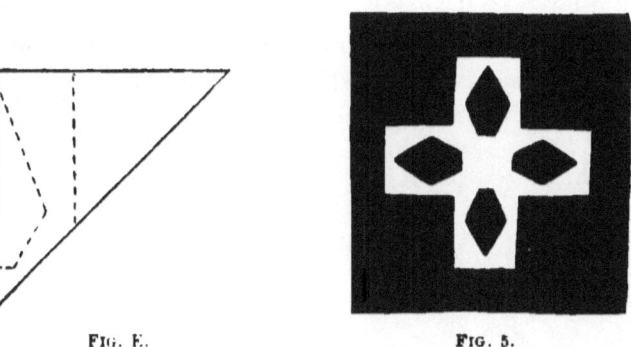

FIG. E.  FIG. 5.

## TERTIARY COLORS.

The Tertiary colors are citrine, olive, and russet. Citrine is a combination of orange and green. Russet — of orange and purple. Olive — of purple and green. Citrine is called the *yellow tertiary*, because *yellow* predominates — being in both the orange and green. Russet — is called the *red tertiary*, as *red* predominates. Olive — the *blue tertiary*, as *blue* predominates.

## CONTRAST AND HARMONY.

*Contrast* must not be mistaken for *harmony*. *Harmony* may include contrast, but, *contrast* to be *harmonious*, must always be *delicate*, never coarse. *Blue* and *Orange* are *complementary colors*, because *each increases* the *brilliancy* of the other, *but* the *violent contrast* offends good taste. *Tints* and *shades* of both colors are often blended with harmonious effects, but children should use simpler combinations.

# THE HEMISPHERE.

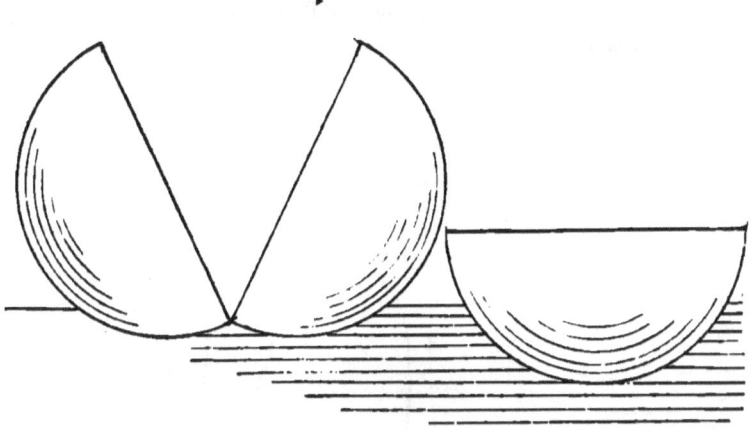

## THE HEMISPHERE.

The teacher will show to the children *two hemispheres*, so placed, as to form a sphere.

Separate them, and ask the children to name them—the natural reply will be, "half of a sphere."

Give the proper name — *hemisphere.*

Now, distribute hemispheres to the class, and ask the children to describe them. They will see that the hemisphere has one plane face and one curved face. The plane face is a circle.

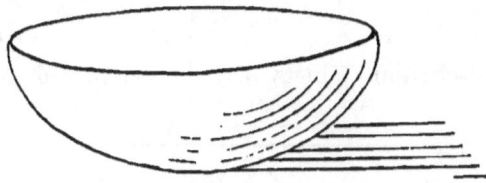

The *clay hemisphere* is formed by cutting the clay sphere in halves.

## THE HEMISISPHERE.

Model *clay objects* resembling the hemisphere — as a hat, a half apple, or a fruit dish.

Have the children find the tablet like the plane face of the hemisphere (circle).

Direct the children to hold the hemisphere on a level with the eye, the *plane face downward* and find *tablet* like this view. Give the name — *semi-circle.*

These semi-circular tablets may be so placed as to form a border.

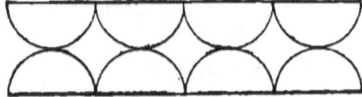

Place *semi-circles* around the sides of a square, and of an oblong — to make a *quatre-foil*.

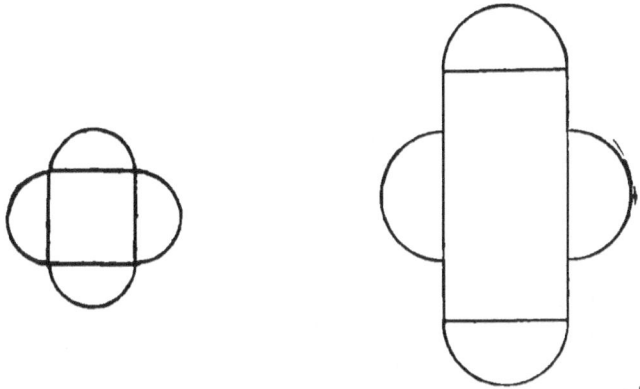

CLAY TRACINGS.— The teacher may cut from cards, various forms, resembling the semi-circle, and let the children place the forms on clay tablets, and trace around the edges. Good subjects may be selected from the tablet forms already mentioned, to which may be added — the side view of an open umbrella, and mouse-trap and mouse.

## THE HEMISPHERE.

These same clay and tablet forms may be pricked on cards, to be sewed by the children.

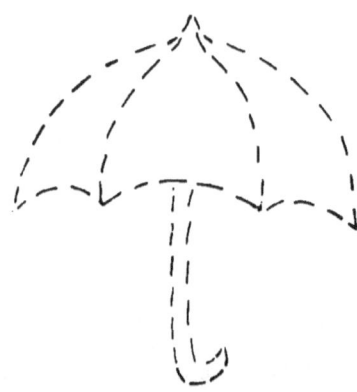

SEWING CARD.

The children having now received these various impressions of semi-circles, in clay, card, and sewing, should give expression, by paper-folding, and drawing, to their knowledge of this form.

PAPER-FOLDING.— Cut a circle (See page 28, Fig. 17) and then cut it in halves (semi-circle). Fold a four-inch paper square to find the *diameters*, and upon them draw semi-circles.

Repeat these *semi-circles*, by *drawing free hand*, both the diameters and curves.

The children may now draw free hand, simple objects having the form of the hemisphere. Draw also upon clay tablet.

DESIGNS. — A practical application of the form study, may now be made by the children in making the following design.

THE HEMISHHERE. 61

Upon a square of red paper draw the *quatre-foil*, as in Fig. 1.

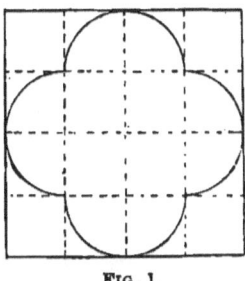

FIG. 1.

Cut out the *quatre-foil*.

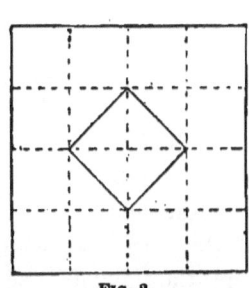

FIG. 2.   FIG. 3.

Upon a square of black paper (of same size as Fig. 1) draw Fig. 2.

Cut out the *central drawing* and place it in the centre of the quatre-foil, mounting the figure thus formed, upon a black or neutral ground. (See Fig. 3).

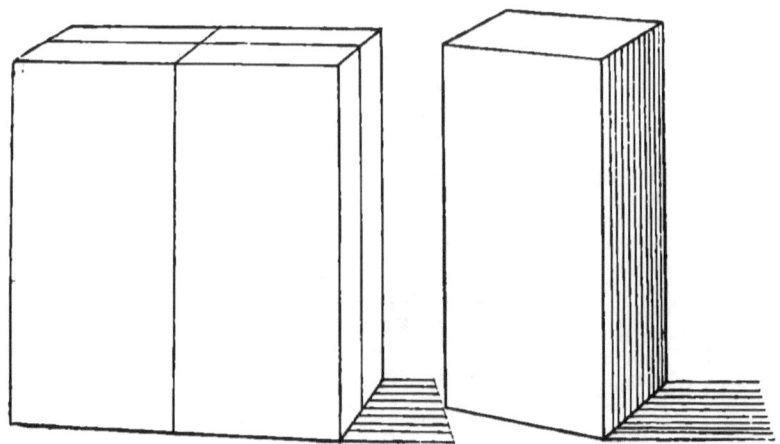

## SQUARE PRISM.

The teacher will hold up before the children, a *cube* composed of four *square prism* solids, and then separate the blocks, to demonstrate that the *square prism* is *one-fourth* of the *cube*.

Then, direct the children to model the *clay cube*, which they are to cut *vertically*, *into quarters* and thus obtain the *square prism*.

Distribute the type solid amongst the class and ask the children to describe the faces and angles. (Four equal oblongs and two squares).

The children may form a *square prism* from a *clay cylinder* by *flattening* the *curved surface*, into *four oblongs* of equal size.

# SQUARE PRISM.

Direct the children to make a paper square prism. First fold a square into sixteen squares, then cut off squares 1, 3, 4, 13, 15, 16.

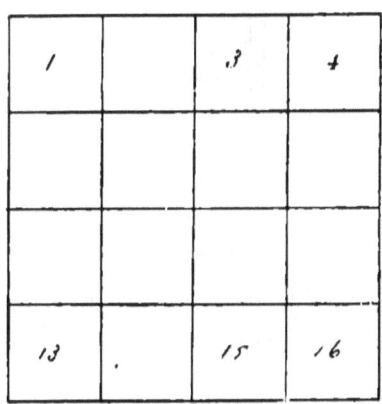

Edges to be joined by sewing or pasting.

A skeleton square prism can be made with *sticks* and *peas*.

## SQUARE PRISM.

Have the children model in clay, objects based upon the *square prism* — as a carpenter's plane, chest, and oblong basket.

Faces of the square prism. The children may find tablets like the faces (four oblongs — two squares).

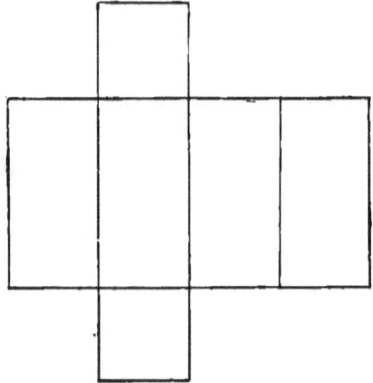

Let the children be *reviewed* by finding the *vertical, horizontal, and parallel edges* and *right angles* of the square prism.

## SQUARE PRISM.

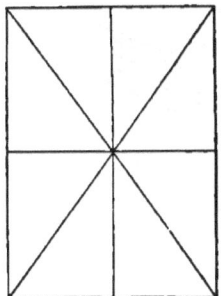

Paper Folding.— Cut a paper oblong — fold for diameters and diagonals — then make an oblong clay tablet of the same size, and mark on it the diameters and diagonals.

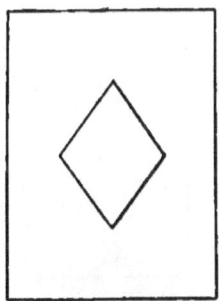

Make another clay tablet of the same size, and draw the *diameters* upon it, place a *point* in the centre of *each half-diameter*, connect the points by lines (to form a *Rhombus*) add more clay to the rhombus, to build it up above the surface of the oblong.

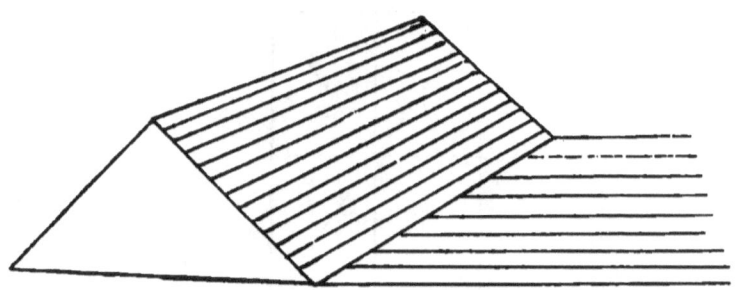

## THE RIGHT-ANGLED TRIANGULAR PRISM.

Let the children mould a clay *square prism* and *bisect* it *diagonally* to *form* a *Right-Angled Triangular Prism.*

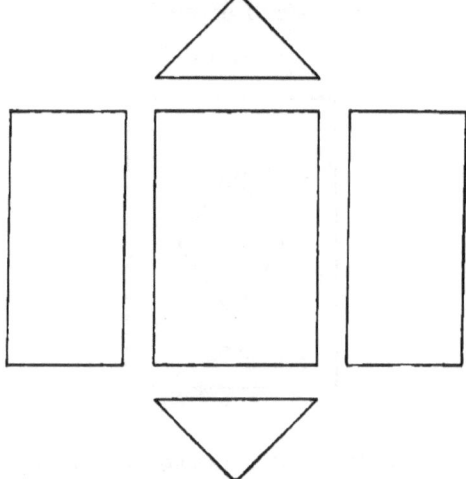

Give the type solid to the class to study, and compare with the clay. They will find *five plane faces*, three oblongs (one wider than

# RIGHT-ANGLED TRIANGULAR PRISM.

the others) and two TRIANGLES. Let the children describe the *triangular face* as to its sides and angles.

With an open pen-knife, the teacher may illustrate the three angles of the triangle.

Give the terms *triangle* and *acute-angle*.

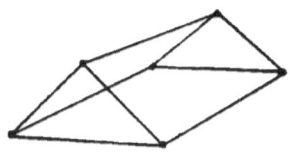

The right-angled triangular prism may also be modeled from the clay cylinder, by flattening the cylinder upon three sides, remembering to finish one face broader than the others.

Have the children mould a clay square prism, and a clay right-angled triangular prism of the same length. The two prisms properly joined resemble a house,—outline doors and windows on the square prism.

# RIGHT-ANGLED TRIANGULAR PRISM.

Find tablets like the faces of the triangular prism and form designs.

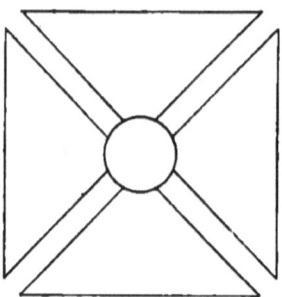

Let the children cut planes from the clay triangular prism, and also cut the the same forms from paper.

A right-angled triangle can be cut from paper, by bisecting a square diagonally.

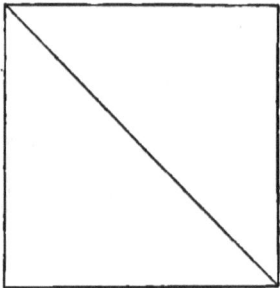

The children should lay sticks for **oblongs** and **triangles**, and then draw the figures.

# EQUILATERAL TRIANGULAR PRISM.

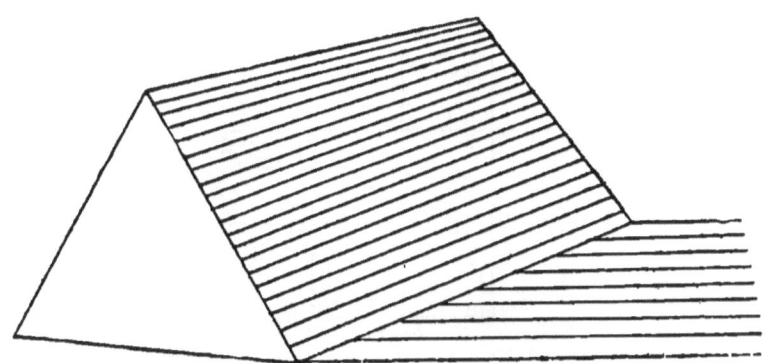

## EQUILATERAL TRIANGULAR PRISM.

The teacher will distribute to the class the type solid square, and equilateral triangular prisms.

By comparison, the children will find that the oblongs are equal in size, in each prism. They will also find that the equilateral triangular prism has but *three* oblong faces, and that the triangular faces have *three equal sides.*

Give the name — equilateral triangular prism.

Have the children mould a clay equilateral triangular prism, from a clay cylinder, by flattening the curved surface to form three equal oblongs.

Next, direct the children to make *this* prism from paper — in this manner — fold each side of a square into four equal parts,

# EQUILATERAL TRIANGULAR PRISM.

making sixteen small squares, cut off the lower row of squares, then cut off each *corner square*. (Fig. 1).

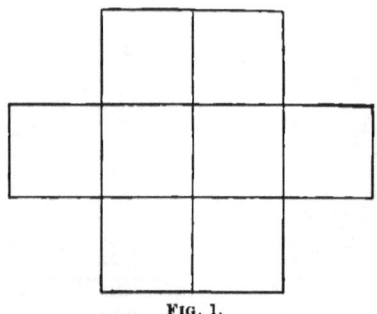

FIG. 1.

Cut the left and right squares to form equilateral triangles. (Fig. 2).

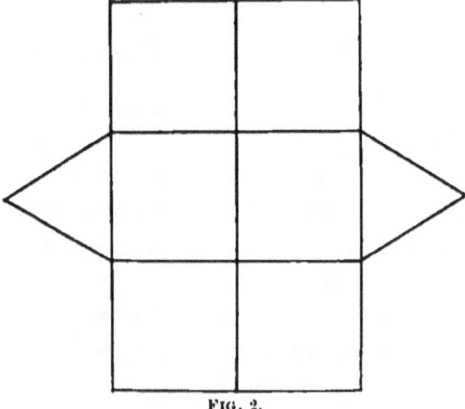

FIG. 2.

Fasten the edges to form an equilateral triangular prism.

## EQUILATERAL TRIANGULAR PRISM.

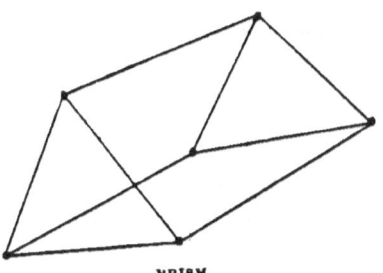 

PRISM.

A skeleton prism may be made with sticks and peas and the children study the edges and corners.

Have the children cut planes from the clay equilateral triangular prism, and *give new term — equilateral triangle.*

Find tablets like the faces of this prism, and arrange in designs.

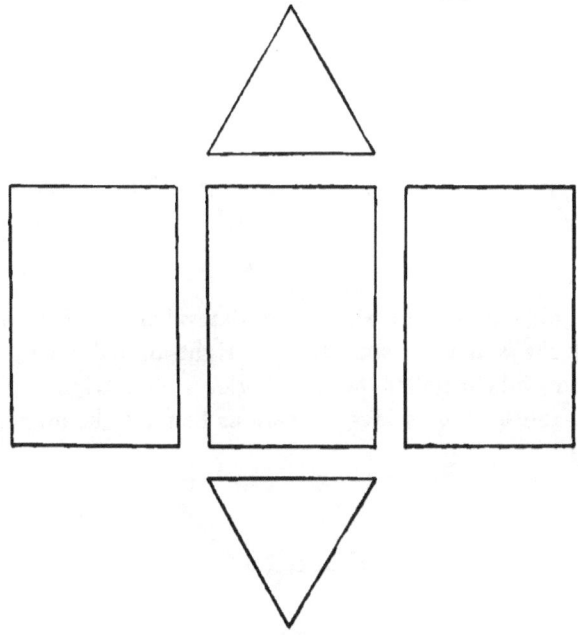

## EQUILATERAL TRIANGULAR PRISM.

Trace the figures on clay, and sew on cards.

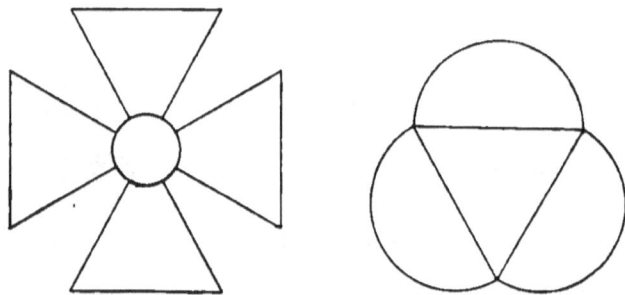

Fold paper to form equilateral triangles. (See Series I. Fig. 22).

Draw these figures:

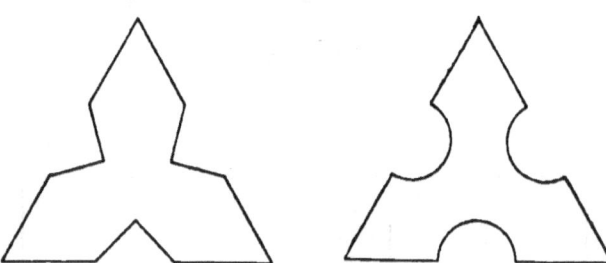

Draw objects based upon the equilateral-triangular prism.

Place the square prism, and the right-angled triangular prism so that the ends form an obtuse angle. Illustrate with an open pen-knife, and let the children lay sticks to form the angle, and then draw it.

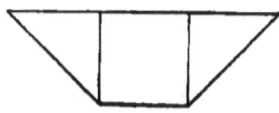

## REVIEW.

At this point it should be ascertained if the children have a clear idea of the type-forms. Without showing the solids the children should be asked to state what they know about their surface — the kind, number, and shape of faces, the edges and corners.

Let the children — from memory — model them of clay, and when practicable make them of paper. Have them draw the faces and views.

Ask them to mould in clay familiar objects which they have not made in school.

Much good will be derived from these review lessons, and possibly marked *latent* talent will be shown. By this means, errors and misunderstandings will be quickly detected. The same test should be applied to *drawing*.

An excellent test in drawing will be found in a dictation exercise — for example, tell the children to think of a square prism, four inches long, two inches wide, and two inches high, resting on the table, and on a level with the eye. Suppose the prism to be in a direct front view, with an oblong face, in a vertical position. *Ask the children to draw the front view.*

Next think of *a cube*, placed on that prism so that the edges and corners of the two solids meet. Add the drawing of the front view of the cube, to that of the prism. Tell the children to imagine the cube *replaced* by an *apple*, and draw that view.

## REVIEW.

After the drawings have been made, show the groups of objects.

Carefully place the objects, so that the views seen by the children, may exactly correspond with the dictation exercise.

## PAPER FOLDING.

A series of *foldings* is here given, which *may* be developed in regular order, although it is better to use each figure after studying the solid from which it is derived. The same method should be followed, as in the first series of paper foldings, *viz.:* Fold and cut from dictation. Next fold and trace outline with lead pencil. Then draw same figure, — testing with ruler. Finally draw free hand upon paper.

Papers used in folding are four inches square.

FIGURE ONE. — Keep paper upon desk, not allowing it to be held in the air when folded.

Fold front edge to meet back edge and left edge of oblong so formed to meet right edge.

Fold upper left corner of square to meet lower right corner.

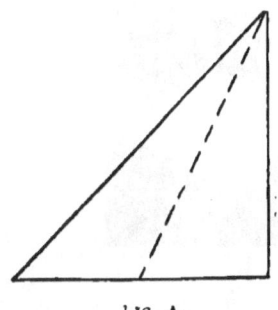
FIG. A.

FIG. 1.

Next fold so crease shall extend from centre of lower side to upper right corner. (Fig. A).

Cut through last fold. Result, (Fig. 1).

PAPER-FOLDING.

Now fold another square just like first one, and instead of cutting, open the square, when the outline of star will be seen.

Let children trace with pencil.

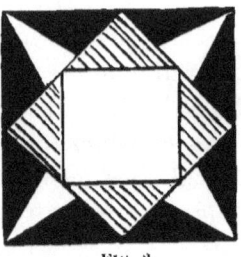

FIG. 2.

FIGURE TWO. — Fold and cut as in Fig. 1.

Fold another square to obtain inscribed square. (See first series, Fig. 12).

Cut out inscribed square and place over star.

Fold another square upon its diameters and cut out one of the small squares. Place this upon the square on the star as in Fig. 2.

 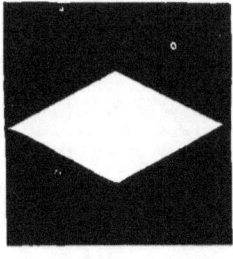

FIG. B.          FIG. 3.

FIGURE THREE. — Use oblong 4x2 inches, or one-half of four inch square. Place on desk, long edges vertical. Fold front edge to meet back edge. **Left edge to meet right edge.**

Cut from lower right corner to upper left corner. (Fig. B. Result, Fig. 3).

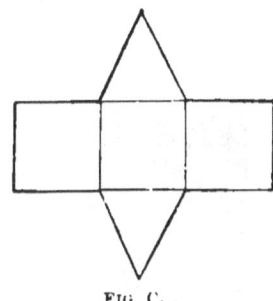

FIG. C.

FIG. 4.

FIGURE FOUR. — Divide square into thirds vertically and horizontally. Cut out each corner square. Cut upper and lower squares into triangles. (See Fig. C). Fold to form envelope (Fig. 4).

FIGURE FIVE. — Cut equilateral triangle. (Series 1, number 22).

Place it with base horizontal on front of desk.

Fold left angle to meet right angle. Fold lower right angle to meet upper angle. Fold left angle to meet right angle.

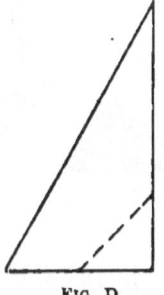

FIG. D.

FIG. 5.

Cut from middle of lower edge to point equally distant from right corner on right edge. (Fig. D. Result, Fig. 5).

78     PAPER-FOLDING.

FIGURE SIX.— Fold triangle as in Fig. 5. Cut from middle of lower edge, in a vertical line to meet left edge. (Fig. E. Result, Fig. 6).

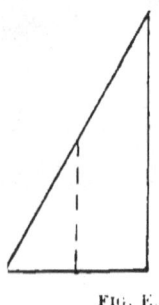
FIG. E.

FIG. 6.

FIGURE SEVEN.— Fold square into small right-angled-triangle

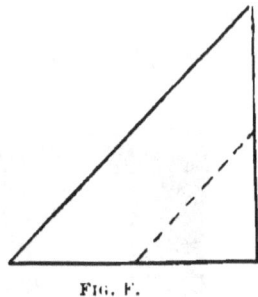
FIG. F.

FIG. 7.

like first part of Fig. 1. Then cut from middle of lower side to middle of right side. (Fig. F. Result, Fig. 7).

PAPER-FOLDING. 79

FIGURE EIGHT.— Fold as for Fig. 7, but cut line curving inward. Fig. G. Result, Fig. 8).

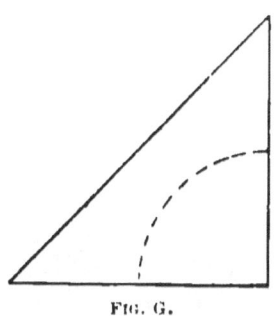
FIG. G.

FIG. 8.

FIGURE NINE.— Fold front edge to meet back edge, and left edge to meet right edge.

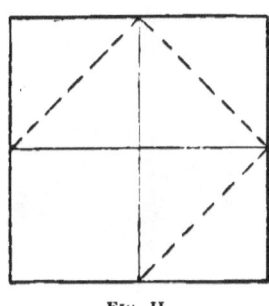
FIG. H.

FIG. 9.

Fold upper left, upper right and lower right corners to meet in centre of square. Fig. H. Cut off corners. Result, Fig. 9).

## PAPER-FOLDING.

FIGURE TEN.—Fold square into right-angled-triangle, and cut in line curving upward from lower right corner to a point on left edge. (Fig I. Result Fig. 10).

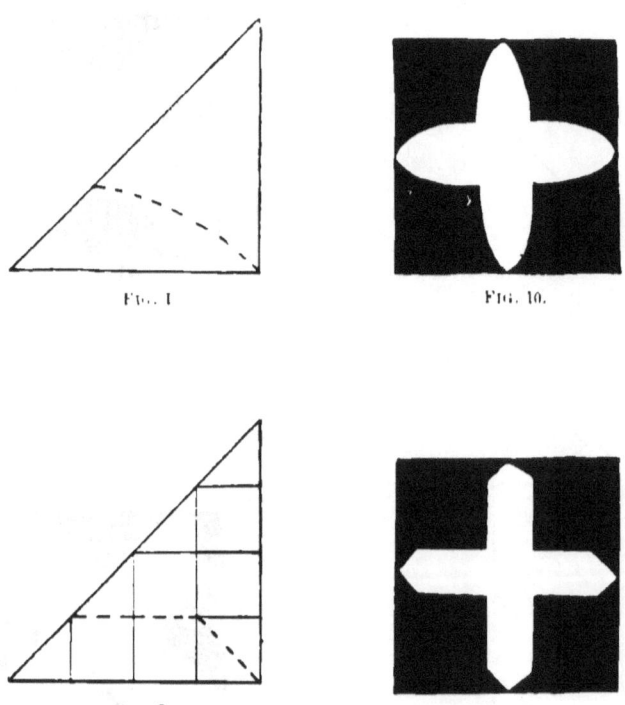

FIG. I.            FIG. 10.

FIG. J.            FIG. 11.

FIGURE ELEVEN.— Fold square into sixty-four small squares. Then into right-angled-triangle, and cut as indicated by dotted line. (Fig. J. Result, Fig. 11).

PAPER-FOLDING.  81

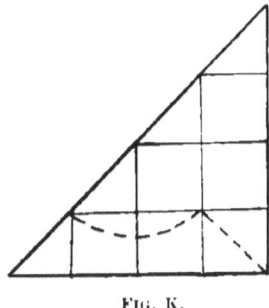

Fig. K.

Fig. 12.

(FIGURE TWELVE.— Fold as for Fig. 11.

Cut curve as per dotted line. (Fig. K. Result, Fig. 12).

Fig. 13.

FIGURE THIRTEEN.— Fold square so it will be divided into thirds. Cut out each corner square. Result, (Fig. 13 or Greek Cross).

82  PAPER-FOLDING.

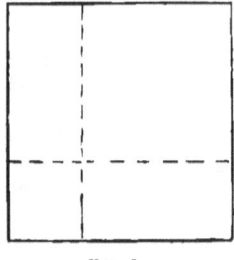

FIG. I.

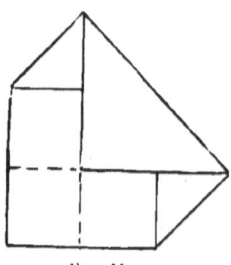

FIG. II.

FIGURE FOURTEEN.— Divide square into thirds. Open square. Fold front edge of square to meet back edge. Fold left edge to meet right edge, (Fig. I.) Fold upper right corner, upper-left corner and lower-right corner as in Fig. II. Cut off these corners. Open paper. (Result, Fig. 14).

FIG. 14.

FIGURE FIFTEEN.— Fold square as for Fig. 1. Cut in a line curving inward from lower-right corner to upper-left corner, (Fig. III). Open paper. (Result, Fig. 15).

PAPER-FOLDING. 83

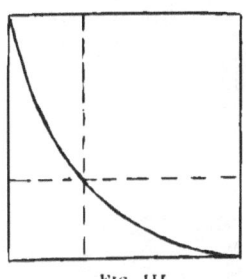

FIG. III.

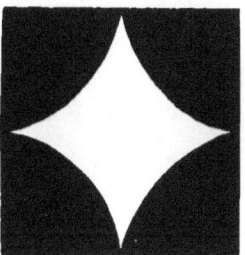

FIG. 15.

FIGURE SIXTEEN.— Maltese Cross. Fold as in Fig. I. Then upper left corner to lower right corner, (Fig. IV.) Cut from middle of right edge to point on left edge which intersects, crease from first fold. Open paper. (Result, Fig. 16).

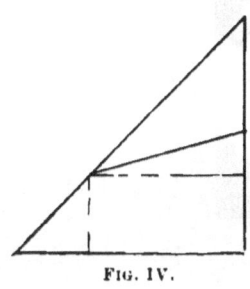

FIG. IV.

FIG. 16.

FIGURE SEVENTEEN. — Cut circle (See Series I. Fig. 17). Cut another square in halves. Place one of the oblongs on desk with short edges horizontal. Fold front edge to meet back edge.

PAPER-FOLDING.

Fold left edge to meet right edge. Cut in line curving outward from lower right corner to upper left corner. Fig. V. Open paper. Result, (an ellipse). Place ellipse so diameters coincide with diameters of circle. (Result, Fig. 17).

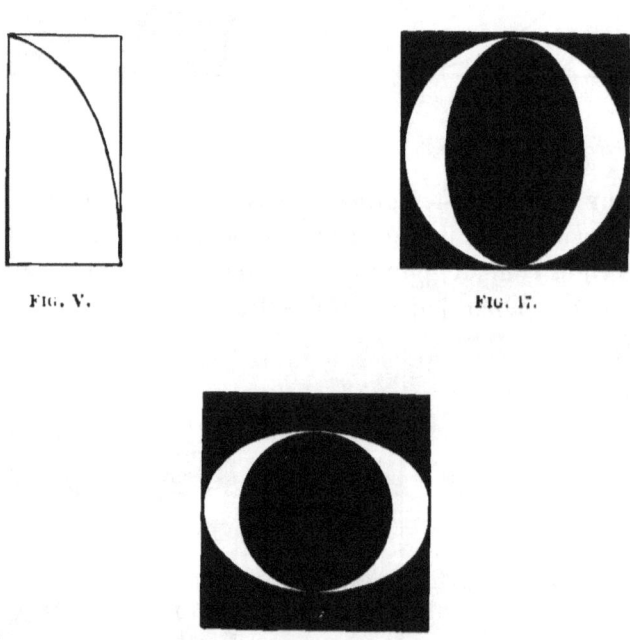

FIG. V.

FIG. 17.

FIG. 18.

FIGURE EIGHTEEN.— Cut ellipse as in Fig. 17. and cut circle from one-fourth of large square. Place the circle upon the ellipse as in Fig. 18.

PAPER-FOLDING.   85

FIGURE NINETEEN.— Cut circle four inches in diameter. Fold edges together till circle is divided into eighths, (Fig. VI). Fold curved edges as in line *a, b*. Open last fold. Cut from point *b* to centre of line *a, b*. Then cut in line curving upward to point *c*. (Fig. VI). Open paper. (Result, Fig. 19).

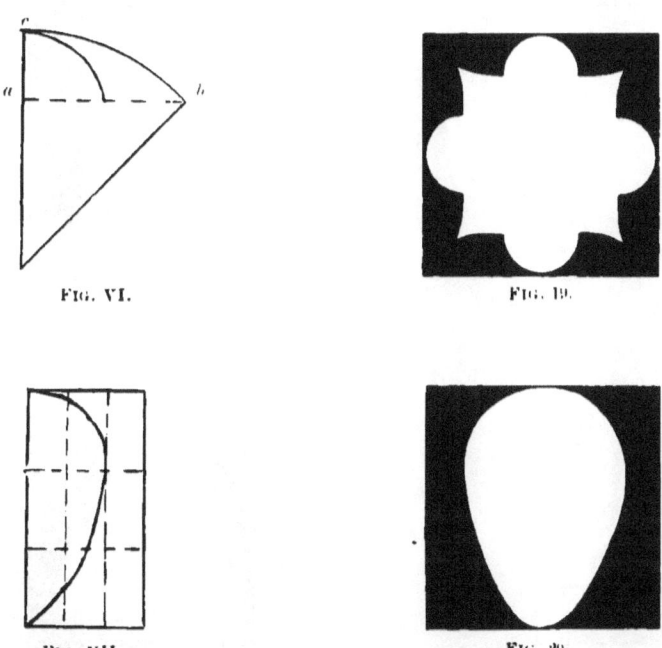

FIG. VI.

FIG. 19.

FIG. VII.

FIG. 20.

FIGURE TWENTY.— Oval. Divide square into thirds. Open paper. Fold left edge to meet right edge. Cut in a curved line from lower left corner to upper left corner, (Fig. VII). Open paper. (Result, Fig. 20).

PAPER-FOLDING.

FIGURE TWENTY-ONE.— Axis of symmetry. Fold an oblong as in Fig. V. Cut from centre of lower edge to centre of right edge, then to upper left corner. Fig. VIII. Open paper. (Result, Fig. 21).

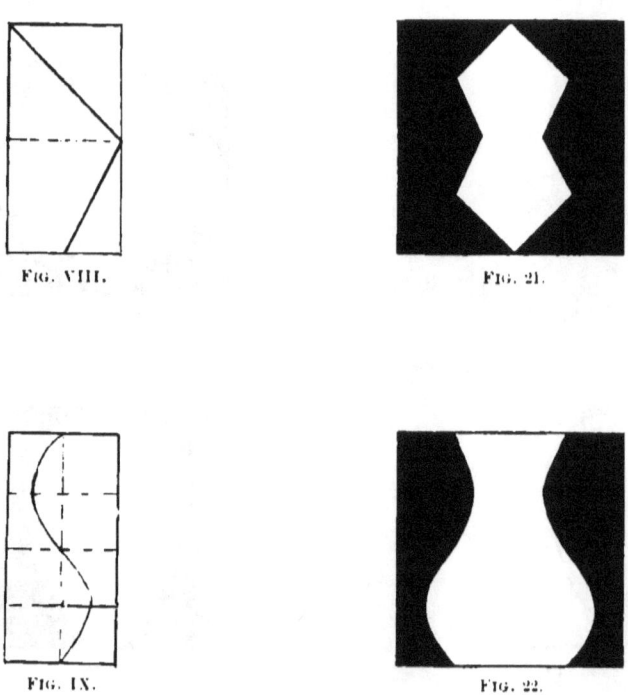

FIG. VIII.

FIG. 21.

FIG. IX.

FIG. 22.

FIGURE TWENTY-TWO.— Fold squares into fourths both ways. Open paper. Fold left edge to meet right edge. Cut as indicated by curved lines Fig. IX. Open paper. (Result, Fig. 22).

PAPER-FOLDING. 87

FIGURE TWENTY-THREE.— Fold square so it is divided into thirds. Open paper. Fold left edge to right edge, and cut as in Fig. X. Open paper. (Result, Fig 23).

FIG. X.

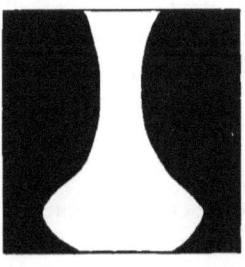

FIG. 23.

FIG. XI.

FIG. 24.

FIGURE TWENTY-FOUR.— Fold as for Fig. X. and cut as in Fig. XI. Open paper. (Result, Fig. 24).

During these paper-foldings, the children have learned to divide the squares into halves, thirds and fourths; and now, the dictation may be assisted, by using the terms — *bisect, trisect,* and *quadrisect.*

The *facts* of proportion, and symmetry, should be presented: for example, give the children an oblong paper, four inches long, and two inches wide. Let them describe the sides and angles. The short sides are *one-half* the length of the long sides. The long sides are *twice* the length of the short sides. Fold for the diameter, by *bisecting* the sides. The divisions must be equal, and the proportions even. *Bisect each half diameter,* thus *quadrisecting* the *entire* diameter.

Connect these points, and see that the different portions of the figure, balance each other.

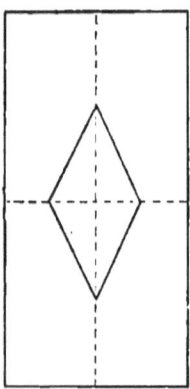

Many dictation lessons should be given upon the forms already studied, as well as upon *new figures,* containing the same principles. Not only for the purpose of furnishing variety, in the methods of impressing *facts,* but also to ascertain the ability of the children to express what they have learned.

## DIMENSIONS.

The children have studied *solids*, as *wholes*, their faces, and edges — also representations of them, by foldings and drawings.

The *paper* used thus far, has been of uniform size (4 inches) and the children should have, by this time, a clear idea of a four-inch square, and of its proportions in halves, quarters and thirds.

Attention should now be given to the study of the *inch*. *Paper-folding* is one of the best methods to use in teaching it, and the figures may be repeated by drawing from dictation — as for example, fold a four-inch square, so that it will be divided into sixteen small squares. (See Fig. 1). Open paper. Each square measures one inch.

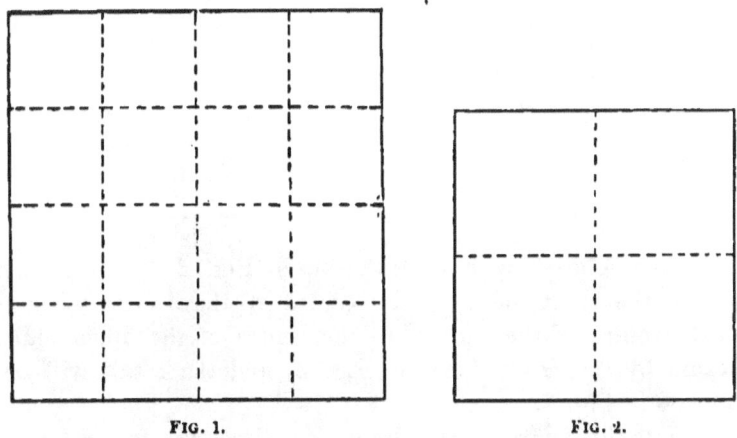

FIG. 1.    FIG. 2.

Cut the squares apart, and study the length and width. Draw the same square from *dictation*.

Fold another paper, as described in Fig. 1, and then, fold the front edge to meet the back edge, and the left edge, to meet the right edge. (See Fig. 2).

From this folding, an almost endless variety of foldings may be formed.

When dictating for drawing, sometimes give a portion of the figure, covering only one-fourth of the surface, and direct the children to complete the figure, by drawing the other parts. Symmetry will thus be taught, and also one of the *fundamental principles* of *design, viz.*: the repetition of a unit.

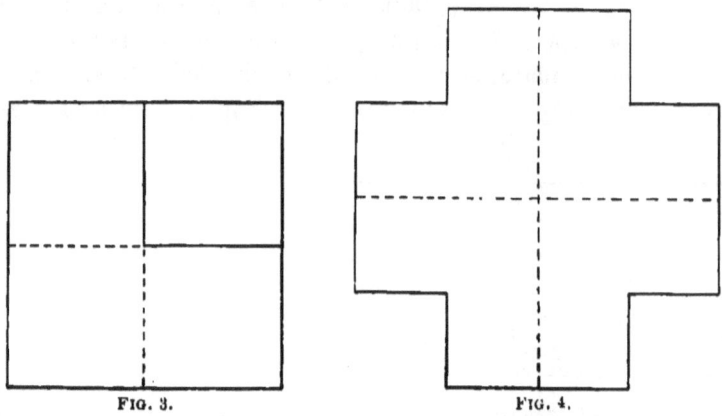

FIG. 3.    FIG. 4.

Having folded paper as described in Fig. 2. Cut from the centre of the right side, to the centre of the square — also cut from the centre of the square, to the centre of the upper side, as indicated by the *heavy lines* in Fig. 3, and the result will be as developed in Fig. 4.

Dictate this figure — first, by giving directions for *each corner*.

Afterward, give directions for *one corner*, and let the children complete the figure.

## DIMENSIONS. 91

This Fig. 5, when developed, gives Fig. 6.

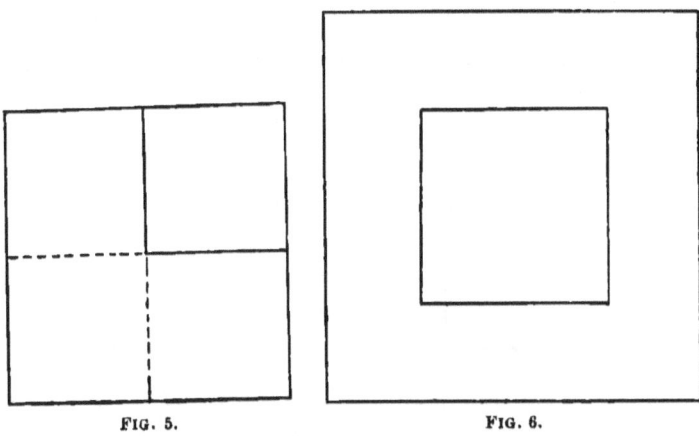

FIG. 5.   FIG. 6.

Another dictation — Fig. 7, developes into Fig. 8.

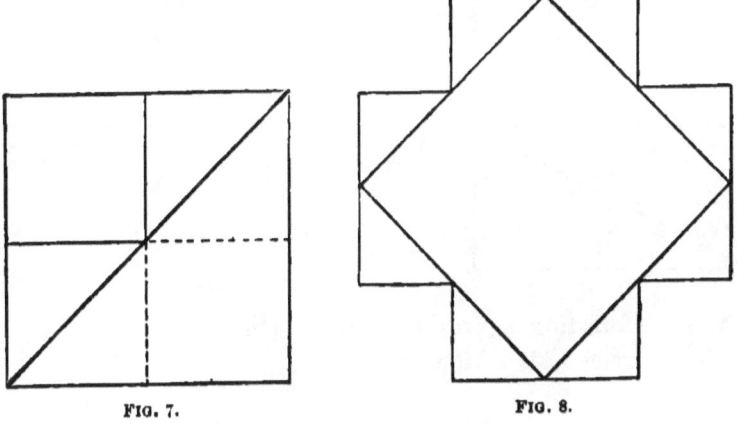

FIG. 7.   FIG. 8.

Another example (Fig. 9) results in Fig. 10.

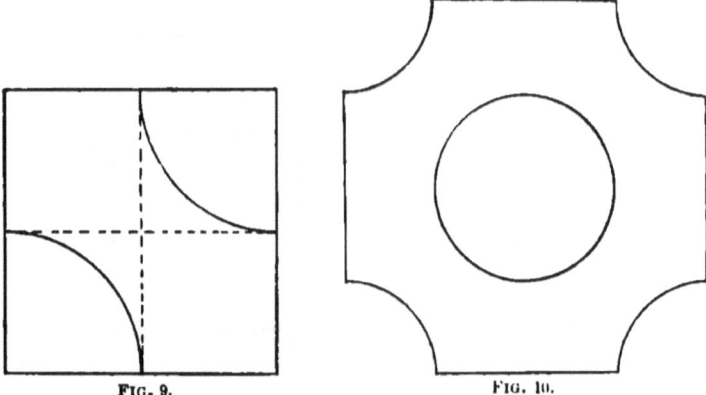

FIG. 9.   FIG. 10.

Again, Fig. 11 develops into Fig. 12.

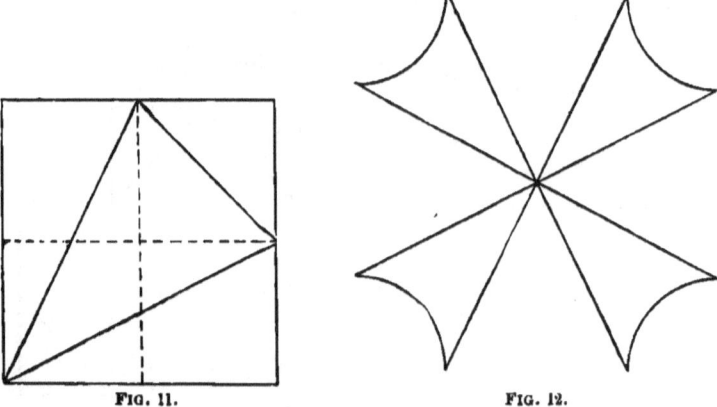

FIG. 11.   FIG. 12.

Many interesting figures may also be made by dividing triangles and circles in like manner.

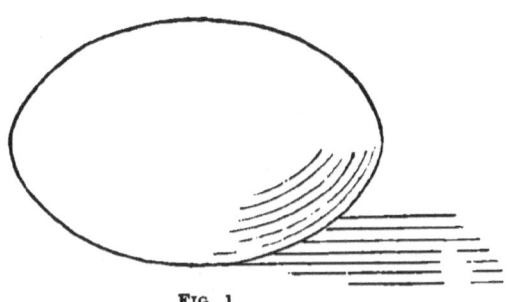

FIG. 1.

## THE ELLIPSOID.

Compare the sphere with the ellipsoid.

The *ellipsoid* has a *curved surface*, but is longer one way than the other. Both ends are alike. Model a *clay ellipsoid*, by first making a sphere, then gradually elongate it, keeping the ends equal, and the entire surface curved. (Fig. 1).

*Clay forms* of objects based upon the ellipsoid, as for example, melon, lemon, potato, banana and cucumber, should also be modeled. (Figs. 2, 3).

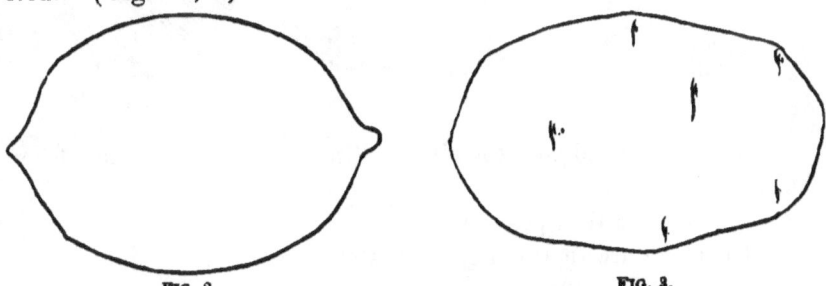

FIG. 2.  FIG. 3.

Next cut the *clay ellipsoid* in halves. (Fig. 4).

## THE ELLIPSOID.

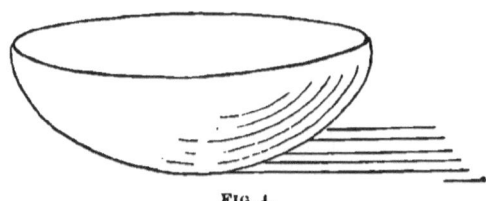

FIG. 4.

Objects based upon the *half ellipsoid* should be modeled as vegetable-dish, turtle, and pods of peas half open. (Figs. 5 and 6).

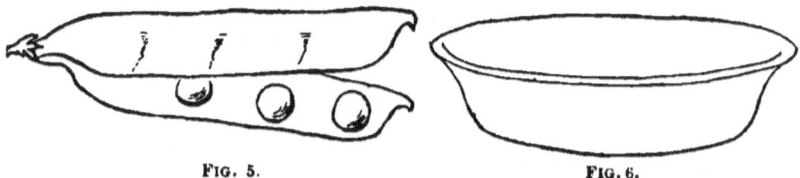

FIG. 5.  FIG. 6.

TABLETS.— Let the children find tablets that represent the views of the ellipsoid. (Figs. 7, 8, 9).

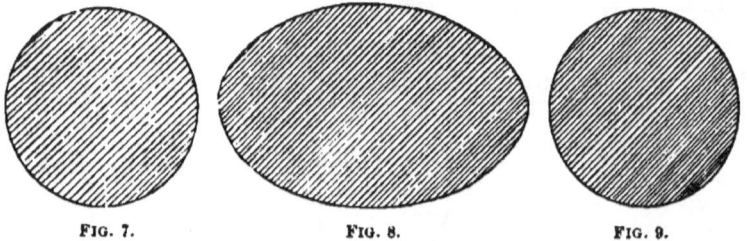

FIG. 7.  FIG. 8.  FIG. 9.

Have each child hold the ellipsoid in a horizontal position, from left to right.

Also in a vertical position.

The views are represented by the ellipse.

Give name — the ellipse.

## THE ELLIPSOID.

Then direct the class to look at the ends of the ellipsoid.
These views are represented by the circle.
Tablets may be arranged to represent groups of elliptical solids, as plums and barberries.

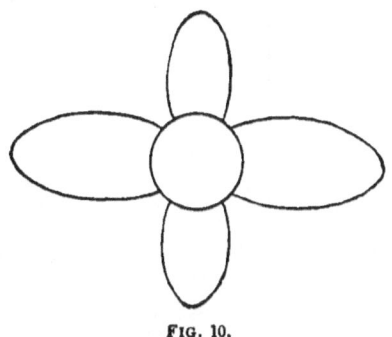

FIG. 10.

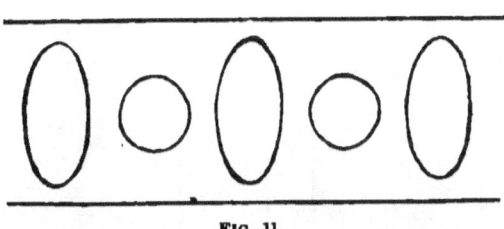

FIG. 11.

Let the children cut a plane from the centre of the clay ellipsoid, showing the ellipse.
Let them paste paper ellipses in simple designs. (Figs. 10 and 11).

## THE ELLIPSOID.

FIG. 12.

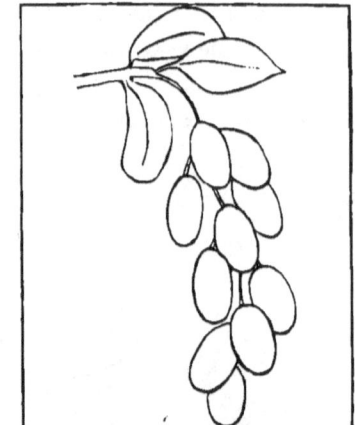

FIG. 13.

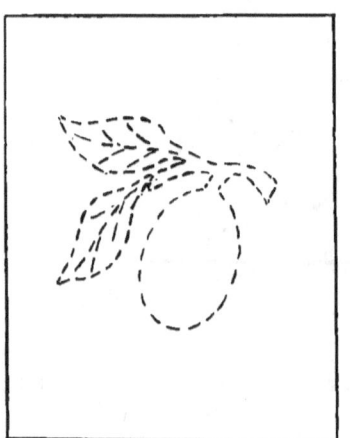

FIG. 14.

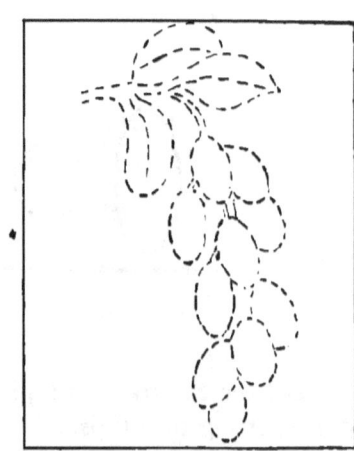

FIG. 15.

# THE ELLIPSOID.

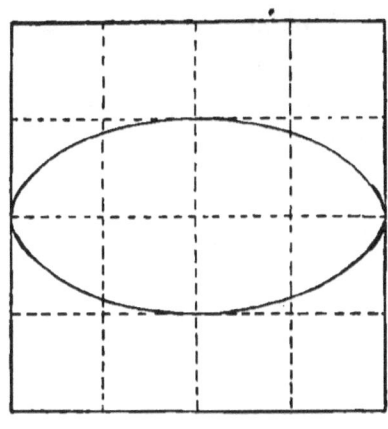

FIG. 16.

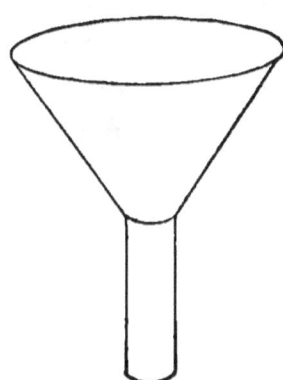

FIG. 17.

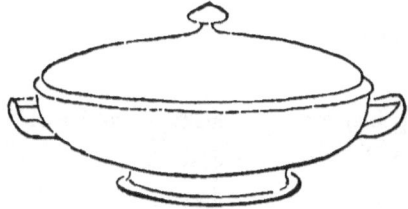

FIG. 18.

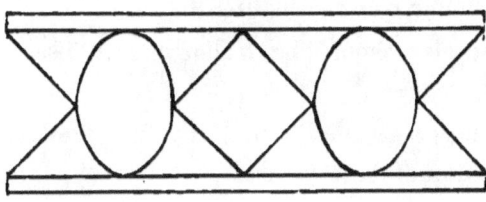

FIG. 19

## THE ELLIPSOID.

Let the children trace the outline of objects upon clay, as leaves, lemon, or plum and branch. (Figs. 12 and 13).

These figures may also be sewed on cards. (Figs. 14 and 15).

They are now ready to cut the ellipse from paper (See page 84, Fig. V).

Follow the four steps as given in directions (See page 75).

---

The *drawing* of the *ellipse* should now be practiced. In drawing a verticle ellipse, hold the pencil as in drawing a circle.

In drawing a horizontal ellipse, hold the pencil with the point upward.

Objects of elliptical form should now be drawn by the children, as the lemon, potato, leaf, cup; a cylinder, tipped so that the upper end appears to be elliptical, and other similar objects. (Figs. 16, 17, 18).

Leaves and flowers of elliptical forms, should be studied and drawn. Also simple conventionalized forms.

Plaques of clay should be made, and ellipses drawn upon them.

A *border* drawn accurately, and cut out of *colored paper*, is a pleasing application of these forms.

# THE OBLATE SPHEROID.

## THE OBLATE SPHEROID.

The study of the *oblate spheroid* should follow the ellipsoid — as many objects which are familiar to the children, are based upon it.

Let the children make a *clay sphere* — and press it lightly between the hands, to *increase* the *horizontal circumference*, and *diminish* the *vertical circumference*, while carefully *preserving* the *curved surface*.

Objects based upon this solid — are the turnip, tomato, doorknob, balls of twine and certain dishes, as above.

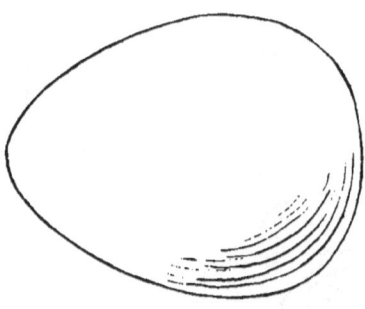

## THE OVOID.

Ask the children to compare the *ovoid* with the *ellipsoid*. They will notice that one end is smaller than the other.

Direct the class to mould a *clay sphere* and to roll it between the palms of their hands until the sphere has been gradually lengthened, and one portion of it has become somewhat pointed. Then shape and smooth the clay, till a *perfect ovoid* is formed. Objects based upon the ovoid are pears, acorns, strawberries, a duck, clover blossom, or the body of the stork.

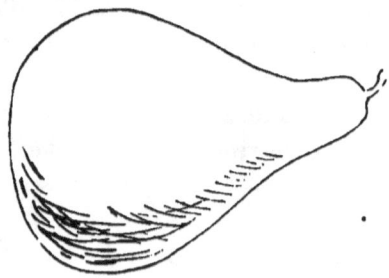

Children should now make *clay plaques* and upon them build up *bas-relief designs.*

Let them begin this line of work by moulding three acorns,

place them in a graceful cluster upon the plaque and complete the design by adding the stem and leaves.

Make another clay plaque, and *draw* the *outline* of the *acorns* on its surface, and gradually build up with little pieces of clay, *within the outline*, until the acorn is formed. Complete the design.

On another plaque, build up the body of the stork, in the same manner.

Sprays of flowers, and leaves, also, are suitable subjects for *bas-reliefs*.

The four oval petals of the syringa can be easily moulded by the children.

From the *half-ovoid*, we obtain the model for a spoon, a mouse or a boat.

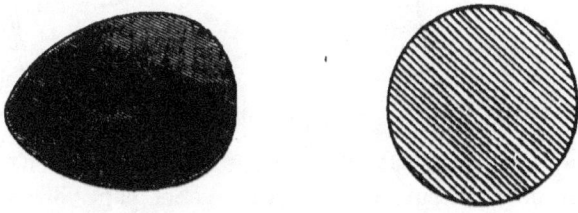

The plane cut from the ovoid is an oval.

Tablets representing views of the ovoid are the oval and circle.

## THE OVOID.

Following the clay work, tablet designs based on the ovals may be made.

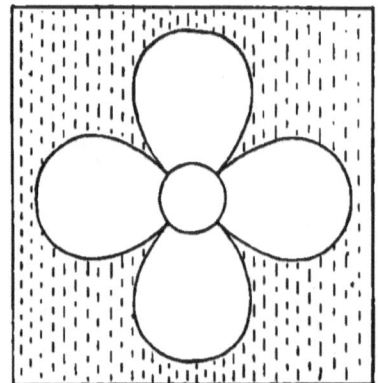

These designs may also be sewed on cards. Next, have the children fold, and cut, a paper oval. (See pages 83 — 85).

Drawing from objects that are oval in form, may now follow.

## THE OVOID.

An egg, a pear, a duck, and the tablet designs previously used are suitable subjects.

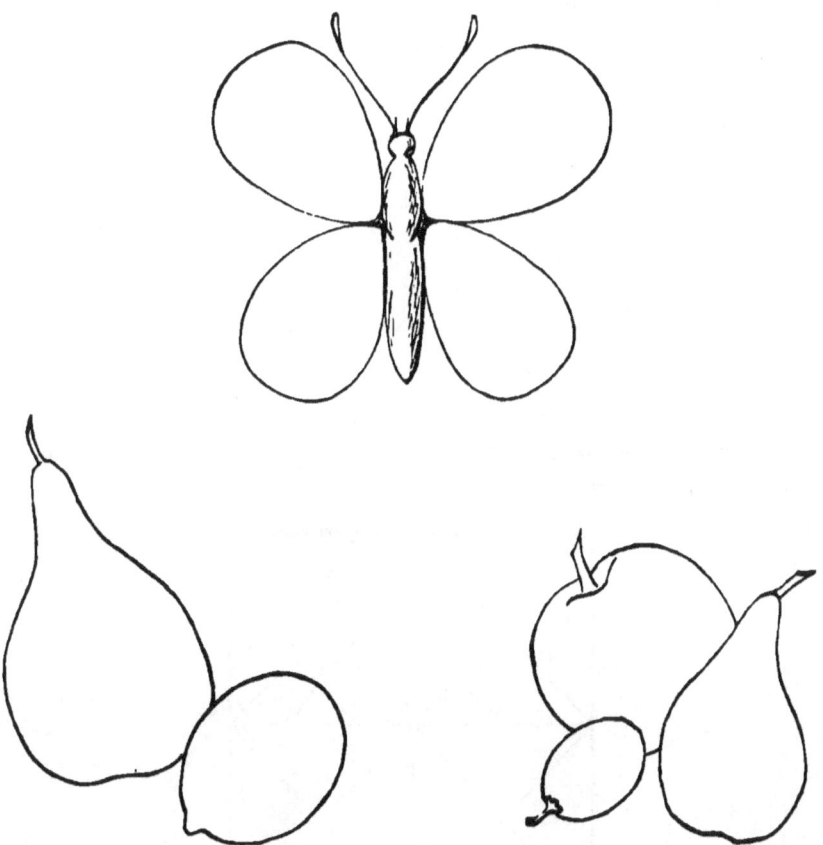

*Groups* of objects may be drawn — for example, a lemon and a pear, or a pear, apple and plum.

## THE OVOID.

Many *vase forms* contain the oval, but before attempting to draw them, the children should be taught the necessity of finishing both sides of the object alike — that the value of the axis of symmetry may be recognized.

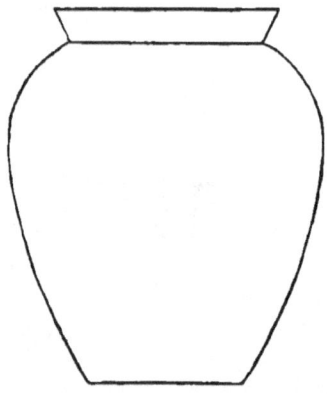

The oval may be introduced into designs for covering a surface, and also in borders.

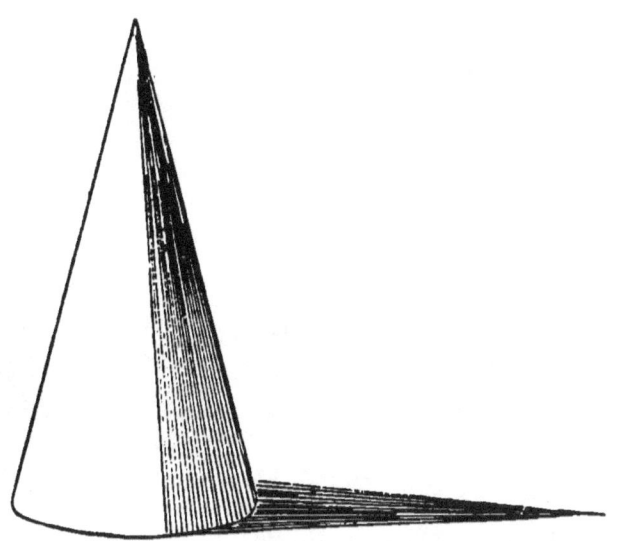

## THE CONE

Let the children name the solid having a base similar to the cone — the *cylinder*. Ask them to roll the two solids (cone and cylinder) on their desks, that they may observe the difference of action.

Give the terms — *base* and *vertex*.

Let the children mould a clay cone — by making first a sphere — then roll it slightly, as for a cylinder, but gradually tapering it at one end. Have the children roll the type solid on their desks, and that action will show them how to roll the *clay*. Objects based upon the cone should also be moulded in clay, as a top, a pine-

## THE CONE.

apple,— tapering roots such as a parsnip or carrot — and certain kinds of shells.

The children may also make a *paper cone*. Divide a square into thirds, by foldings. In the middle square of the lower row,

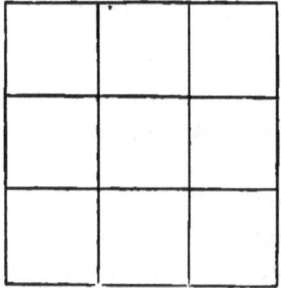

cut a circle having the same diameter as the square, and leave the

## THE CONE.

circle attached to the middle square. Fold back the paper in a line from the middle of the right side of the large square, to the middle of the upper side of the large square. Also fold back from the middle of the left side, to the middle of the upper side. Cut the paper in a curved line from the middle of the right side of

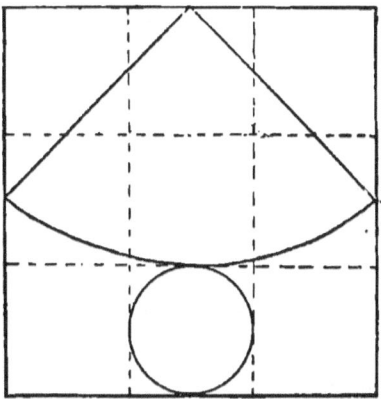

the square,— and also from the left side of the square, to the upper part of the circle. Then cut off the upper left and right corners that were folded back. (See Fig.) Join the edges by sewing — first the slanting edges — then bend up the circle, and join to the hollow cone.

TABLETS.— In finding the tablet resembling the cone, the chil-

## THE CONE.

dren will discover a *new triangle*. Let them describe it and give the name — *isosceles triangle*.

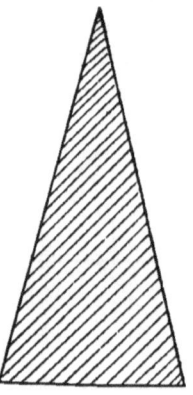

Direct the children to mould a clay cone, and then cut it vertically. Let them describe the plane faces. They will recognize the *semi-circle*.

The *triangular face* may be cut from an *oblong*, whose width equals the diameter of the base of the cone, and whose length equals the height of the cone. Fold the oblong vertically, left edge to meet the right edge, and cut a slanting line from the lower right corner to the upper left corner.

# THE CONE.

Let the children study the views of a cone and draw them.
The plane face, or bottom view, is a circle.
The top view is a circle with a point in the centre for a vertex.

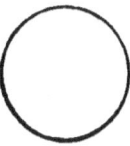

In the front view, be sure the vertex of the triangle is over the centre of the base.

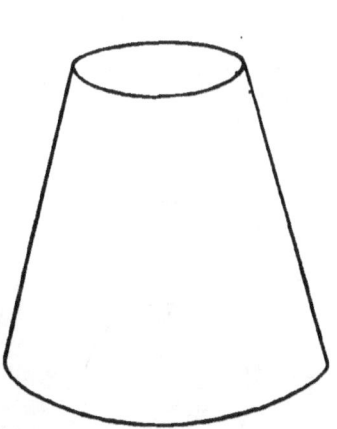

## THE TRUNCATED CONE.

Let the children mould a clay cone, and cut through it parallel to the base. Teach the name — *truncated cone*. A flower pot, tumbler or basket may be moulded from this cone.

## 112    THE TRUNCATED CONE.

Let the children draw the top view of the *truncated cone*, producing the concentric circles —

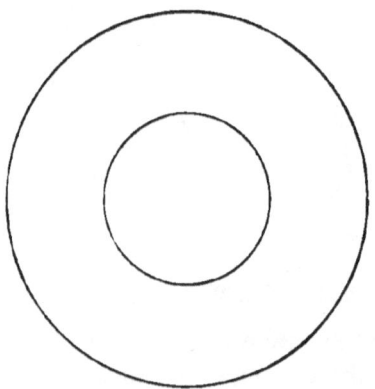

# THE SQUARE PYRAMID.

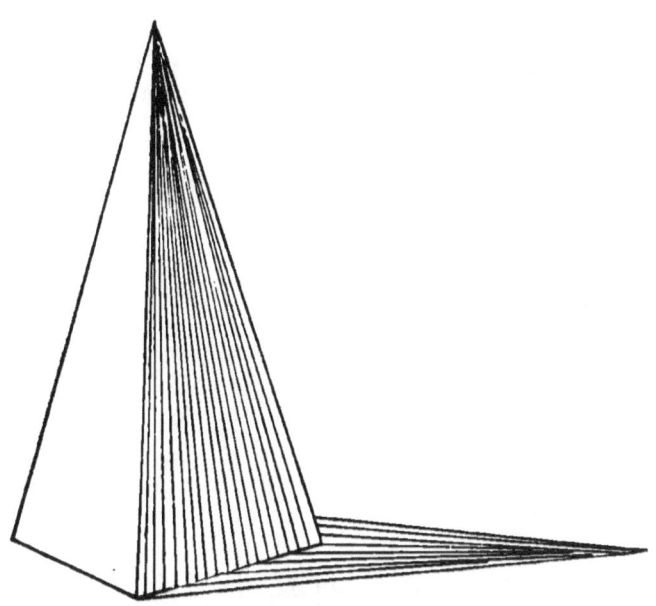

## THE SQUARE PYRAMID.

The cone and the square pyramid should be compared by the children. Let each child handle the type-solids, and they will discover that both solids have a base and a vertex, and that a *portion* of the surface of the *cone* is *curved*, and the surface of the square pyramid is all plane. Also, that the base of the cone is a circle, and that of the square pyramid is a square. The sides of the **square pyramid** are isosceles triangles.

Direct the children to mould a square pyramid from a **clay cone**

## THE SQUARE PYRAMID.

in this manner: Tap the curved surface of the cone, until four equal triangular faces are made, and the base becomes a square. Be careful to finish the faces with sharp edges.

On one side of a clay pyramid, let the children mark lines and figures to imitate a thermometer — on another insert pegs, imitating a rack.

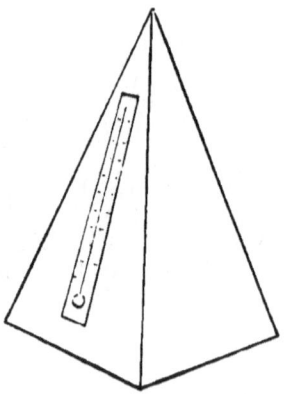

The children should next make a *paper pyramid*.

Divide a *square* into thirds by folding. Then, using the sides of the centre square for bases, cut triangles, as in Fig. 1, page 115.

## THE SQUARE PYRAMID.

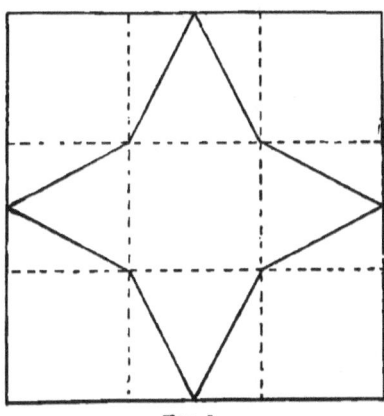

Fig. 1.

Fold the paper so that all the triangles can be cut at once.

---

The *faces* of the *pyramid* should next be studied. Find tablets like the base and front faces of the pyramid.

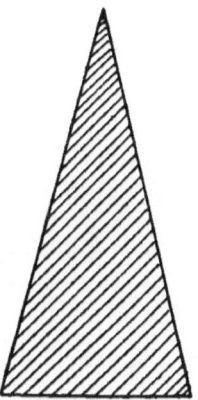

Describe the *square* and *isosceles triangle*.

## THE SQUARE PYRAMID.

Direct the children to place the tablets to represent the pyramid and borders.

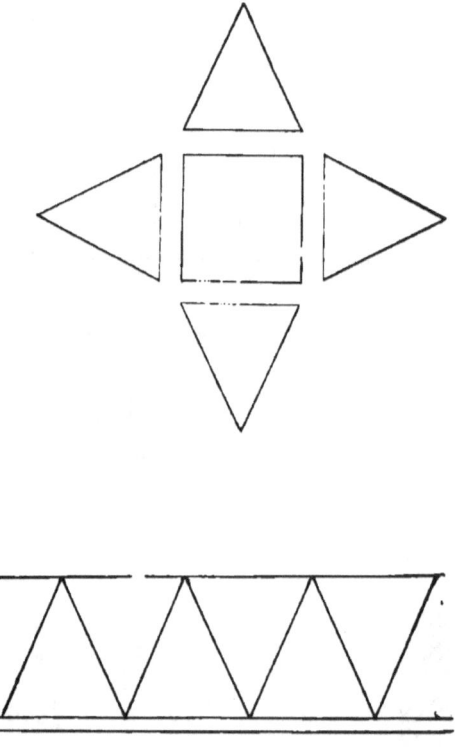

Let the children make a skeleton pyramid of sticks and peas, by making a square base. Then insert a stick in each corner

## THE SQUARE PYRAMID.

in an upright position and join the four uprights with a pea, at the vertex.

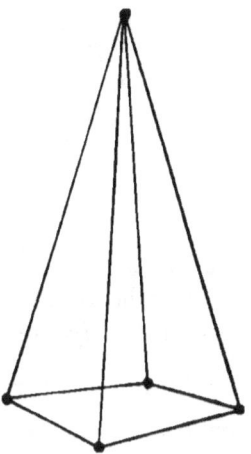

Let the children *bisect*, *vertically*, a clay *pyramid*, and study its faces (triangles and oblong.)

---

VIEWS OF THE PYRAMID. — Let the children draw the bottom view of the pyramid (a square), and then draw the front and side views (isosceles triangles.)

Then direct them to hold the pyramid, with its vertex directly in front of the eye, and draw the top view. (See Fig., next page).

## THE SQUARE PYRAMID.

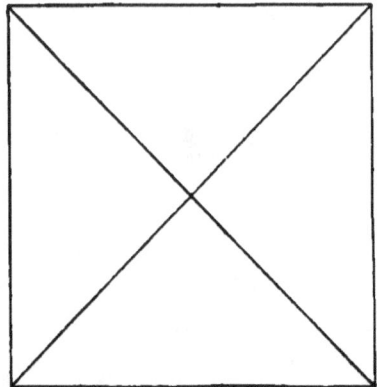

In this drawing, care must be taken to represent the *vertex* by a *point* — and also to represent the *edges* of the *faces*.

---

The children may now *truncate* a clay pyramid, as they did the cone, and also model objects based upon it.

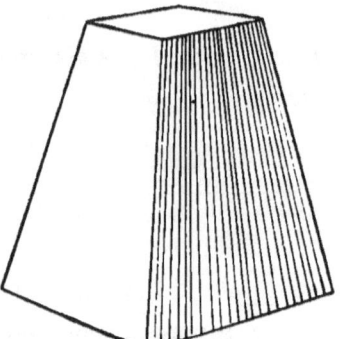

Draw the top view. (See Fig. 1, page 119).
Designs may be made with tablets and drawn. (Figs. 2, 3, 4.)

# THE SQUARE PYRAMID.

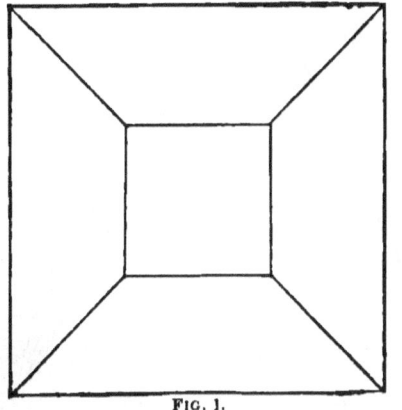

Fig. 1.

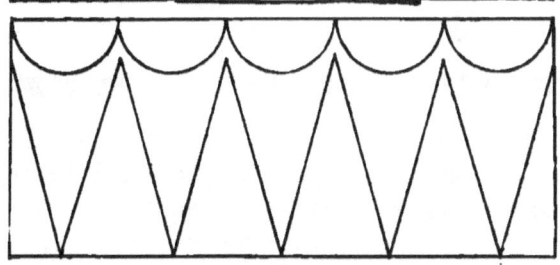

Fig. 2.

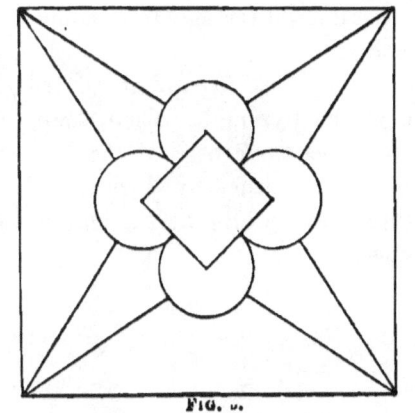

Fig. 3.

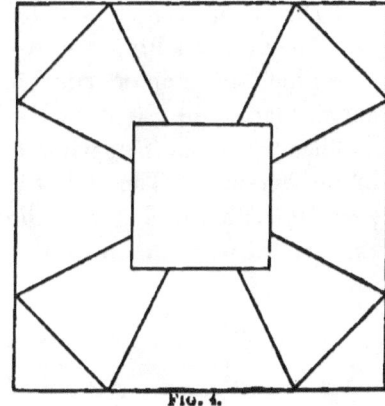

Fig. 4.

## EQUILATERAL TRIANGULAR PYRAMID.

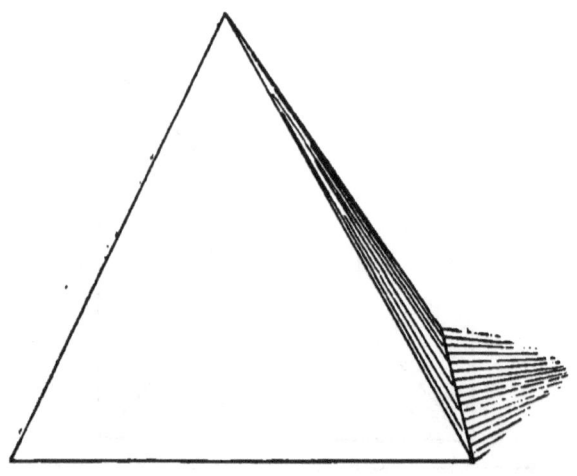

**EQUILATERAL TRIANGULAR PYRAMID.**

Give to the children for comparison — the square pyramid and the equilateral triangular pyramid. They will find that the triangles in the one, are *isosceles triangles*, and *equilateral triangles* in the other — that one has a square base, the other has a triangular base, that the faces on the triangular pyramid are all alike.

Direct the class to model a clay equilateral triangular pyramid. They can readily do so from a sphere.

First, shape one portion of the sphere into an equilateral triangular face, and use it as the base of the pyramid. Then, shape another triangular face with its vertex over the centre of the base of the pyramid. The other two faces can be formed by *shaping* and *pressing* with the fingers, more easily than by tapping the clay on the slate as was done in moulding other models.

## EQUILATERAL TRIANGULAR PYRAMID. 121

A paper pyramid may be made in this manner. Cut an equilateral triangle. (See page 30.)

Then fold each corner, to meet the centre of the opposite side; this gives a central triangle, which forms a base.

Fold the three sides of the large triangle, that the corners may meet in a point and join the edges.

---

Let the children find tablets like the faces, and arrange in designs and draw them.

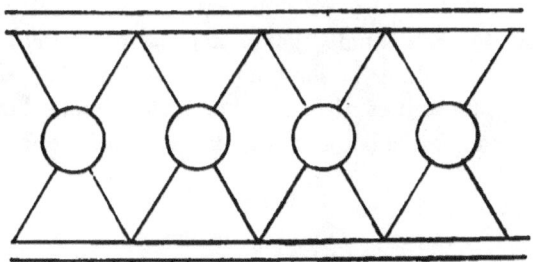

## SUGGESTIONS.

When possible to do so, use clay modeling to illustrate each subject of study.

In the study of birds and animals the distinguishing characteristics of form may thus be taught in a very interesting manner. The roots, leaves, and blossoms of plants may be modeled on plaques.

Language lessons may be illustrated by the children in freehand sketches, after this method:—The teacher may tell the class a story, and while she talks the children should draw, in outline, various objects mentioned by her. These objects should be the same as those previously modeled or drawn.

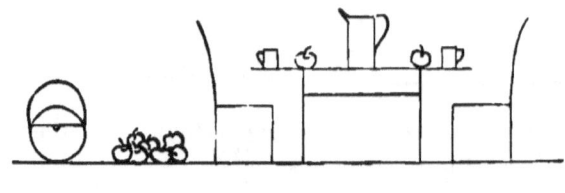

**STORY.**

"Two little girls, Mary and Alice, are playmates and go to the same school.

One day Mary's uncle gave her a round, covered basket with a handle. Wishing to show her present to Alice, she filled the basket with apples and carried it to her little friend's house. After the children had talked about the kind uncle's gift, they began to play. They brought a little table and placed two chairs beside it. Each little girl had an apple, and a mug for milk. In the centre of the table was placed a tin quart measure full of milk. When the children were tired of this, they ran out into the garden to play with a new red balloon that had been given to Alice.

While Alice was running, the wind blew the balloon out of her hand, but the string caught in the clothes line and held it fast.

The children could not reach the clothes-line, even on tip-toe, nor when Alice brought a big square box to stand upon. But she called her brother John, who came with a ladder and soon the runaway balloon was safe in her hands again.

Alice will be more careful next time."

124 CONSTRUCTION WORK IN CARD-BOARD.

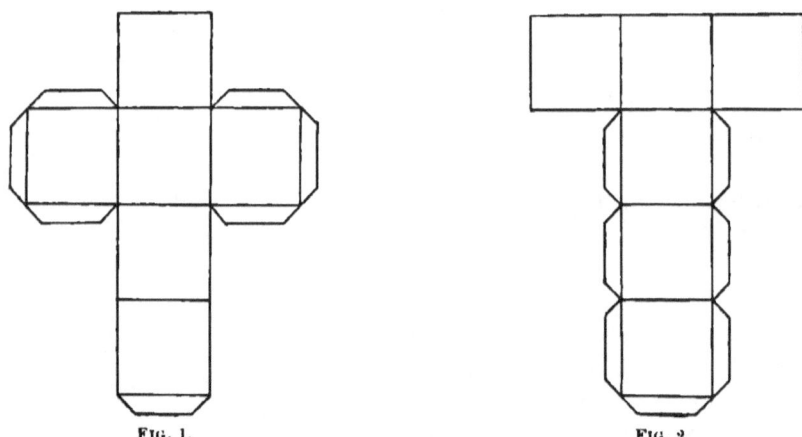

FIG. 1.   FIG. 2.

## CONSTRUCTION WORK IN CARD-BOARD.

Objects that can be firmly constructed by means of laps or margins, should now be made.

They should be based upon the Type-Solids, and may be constructed of *light-weight* card-board. After the plan of the object has been drawn, the outline should be cut out with the scissors, and *where* the card-board is to be *bent*, cut through half its thickness with a sharp knife, similar in shape to a shoe-knife. The card-board should be placed upon a smooth board, and while the left hand firmly holds the iron ruler to the line to be cut, draw the knife lightly downward to avoid cutting through the cardboard.

Use the *blade* in cutting, rather than the point of the knife.

These objects may be made of heavy Manilla *paper*, without the use of the knife, if preferred.

The following suggestions will illustrate this work.

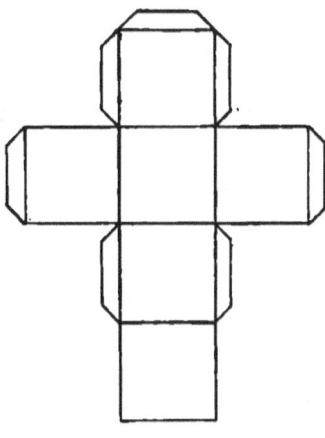

Fig. 3.

## THE CUBE.

There are several ways of drawing the margins of a cube, as may be seen by the above illustrations. Fig. 1. is the simplest. For a two-inch cube, a paper ten inches square is required. With a ruler find the centre of the upper edge of the paper, and place a point there. Place a point one-half inch *below* point 1. With the *last point* as a centre, draw a horizontal line two inches long. From *left* end of horizontal line, draw downward a vertical line eight inches long. From *right* end of horizontal line draw downward a vertical line eight inches long. Connect the lower ends of the vertical lines. Beginning at the upper ends of the vertical lines, place points two inches apart and connect these points by horizontal lines. Extend the *central* horizontal line and the one above it, two inches at *left* and *right* of vertical lines. Connect the left ends with the vertical line, and also the right ends.

Place a margin one-fourth of an inch wide around the *upper*, *left* and *lower* sides of the *left square*. Also around the *upper*, *right* and *lower sides* of the *right square*, and on the *lower* side of the *lower square*. Cut off the corners of each margin, as in Fig. 1. To complete the figure, cut first through the outline; then cut partially through the lines bordered by the margins, and fold into the form of the cube, placing the margins *inside* and paste the edges neatly together. Other designs are given in Figs. 2 and 3.

---

A CUBICAL BOX. Draw the cube again, and place margins *one-fourth of an inch* in width, on the upper and lower edges of the left and right squares, and a *half-inch* margin upon the left, lower and right edges of the lower square.

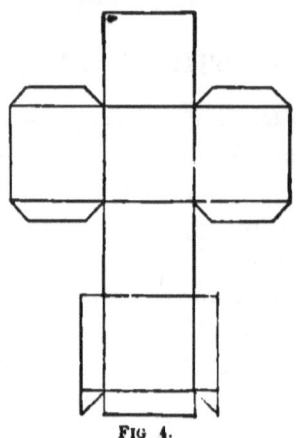

FIG 4.

Cut the corners, as in Fig. 4, and form a box with cover.

# THE CUBE.

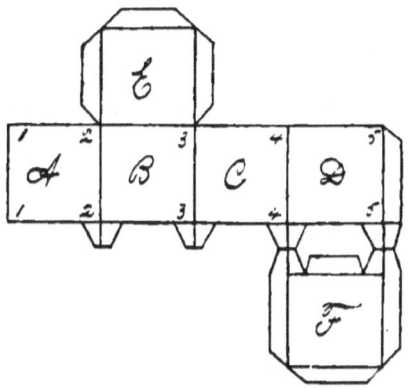

A CUBICAL SAFE.—On the *left edge* of the paper place a point, two and one-quarter inches from the upper edge, and number it 1. From this point, extend a horizontal line, eight and one-quarter inches toward the right. Place *another point* at the left edge of paper, two inches below point No. 1, and from it draw another horizontal line, also eight and one-quarter inches long. On these lines, beginning at the left, place points two inches apart, and number them 2, 3, 4, 5. Connect these points by vertical lines, and mark the squares thus formed A. B. C. D.

Adjoining the upper side of Square B draw another two inch square, and mark it E. Place a quarter-inch margin on the left and right sides of square E. One-half inch below the second horizontal line, draw a third horizontal line, and extend the vertical lines from points 2, 3, 4 and 5 to meet it. On the third horizontal, place points at the right and left of the verticles, one-eighth of an inch distant from each vertical. One the horizontal line above, (the second) place points at the right and left of each vertical, *one-fourth* of an inch distant. Connect *these* points on the second and third horizon-

128    SUGGESTIONS FOR STICK-LAYING.

tal lines, by oblique lines. At the right of the vertical line 5, allow a quarter-inch margin. Draw the door in square D.

Cut out the figure and fold the margins *inside*, and paste neatly.

To add a bottom to the safe, add square F, as in the cut, and paste the margins.

## SUGGESTIONS FOR STICK-LAYING.

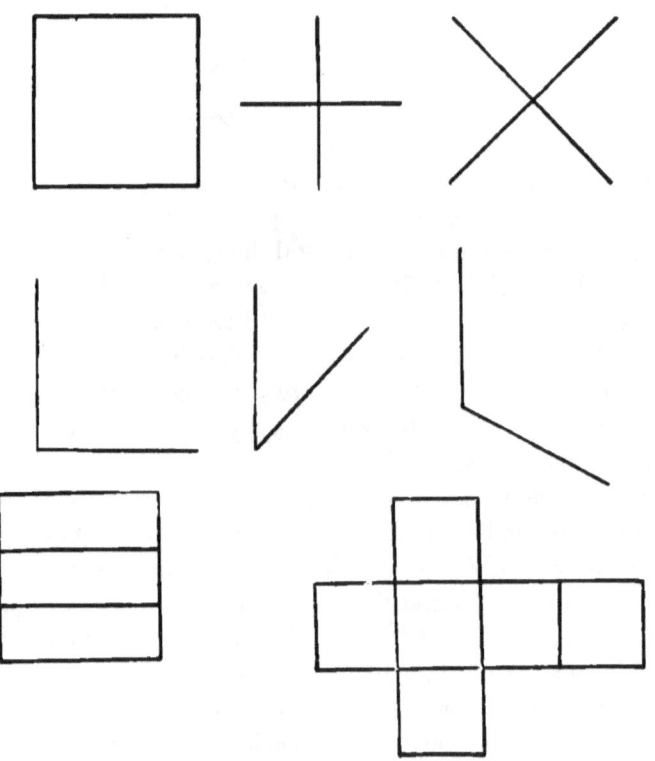

## SUGGESTIONS FOR STICK-LAYING.

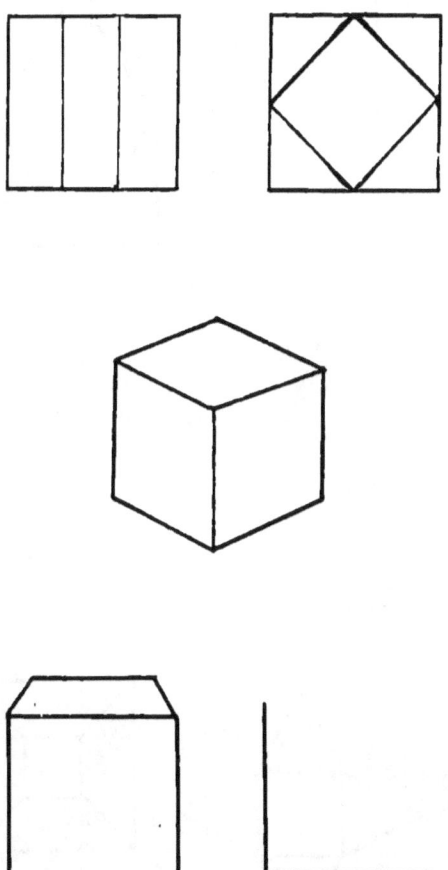

130 SUGGESTIONS FOR STICK-LAYING.

www.ingramcontent.com/pod-product-compliance
Lightning Source LLC
Chambersburg PA
CBHW031618170426
43195CB00037B/1107